This book belongs to:

_____

# Scorpio Daily Horoscope 2024

Mystic Cat
Suite 41906, 3/2237 Gold Coast HWY
Mermaid Beach, Queensland, 4218
Australia
islandauthor@hotmail.com

The information accessible from this book is for informational purposes only. No statement within is a promise of benefits. There is no guarantee of any results.

Images are under license from Shutterstock, Dreamstime, Canva, or Depositphotos.

# Contents

# 2024

## January

| S | M | T | W | T | F | S |
|---|---|---|---|---|---|---|
| | 1 | 2 | 3 | 4 | 5 | 6 |
| 7 | 8 | 9 | 10 | 11 | 12 | 13 |
| 14 | 15 | 16 | 17 | 18 | 19 | 20 |
| 21 | 22 | 23 | 24 | 25 | 26 | 27 |
| 28 | 29 | 30 | 31 | | | |

## February

| S | M | T | W | T | F | S |
|---|---|---|---|---|---|---|
| | | | | 1 | 2 | 3 |
| 4 | 5 | 6 | 7 | 8 | 9 | 10 |
| 11 | 12 | 13 | 14 | 15 | 16 | 17 |
| 18 | 19 | 20 | 21 | 22 | 23 | 24 |
| 25 | 26 | 27 | 28 | 29 | | |

## March

| S | M | T | W | T | F | S |
|---|---|---|---|---|---|---|
| | | | | | 1 | 2 |
| 3 | 4 | 5 | 6 | 7 | 8 | 9 |
| 10 | 11 | 12 | 13 | 14 | 15 | 16 |
| 17 | 18 | 19 | 20 | 21 | 22 | 23 |
| 24 | 25 | 26 | 27 | 28 | 29 | 30 |
| 31 | | | | | | |

## April

| S | M | T | W | T | F | S |
|---|---|---|---|---|---|---|
| | 1 | 2 | 3 | 4 | 5 | 6 |
| 7 | 8 | 9 | 10 | 11 | 12 | 13 |
| 14 | 15 | 16 | 17 | 18 | 19 | 20 |
| 21 | 22 | 23 | 24 | 25 | 26 | 27 |
| 28 | 29 | 30 | | | | |

## May

| S | M | T | W | T | F | S |
|---|---|---|---|---|---|---|
| | | | 1 | 2 | 3 | 4 |
| 5 | 6 | 7 | 8 | 9 | 10 | 11 |
| 12 | 13 | 14 | 15 | 16 | 17 | 18 |
| 19 | 20 | 21 | 22 | 23 | 24 | 25 |
| 26 | 27 | 28 | 29 | 30 | 31 | |

## June

| S | M | T | W | T | F | S |
|---|---|---|---|---|---|---|
| | | | | | | 1 |
| 2 | 3 | 4 | 5 | 6 | 7 | 8 |
| 9 | 10 | 11 | 12 | 13 | 14 | 15 |
| 16 | 17 | 18 | 19 | 20 | 21 | 22 |
| 23 | 24 | 25 | 26 | 27 | 28 | 29 |
| 30 | | | | | | |

## July

| S | M | T | W | T | F | S |
|---|---|---|---|---|---|---|
| | 1 | 2 | 3 | 4 | 5 | 6 |
| 7 | 8 | 9 | 10 | 11 | 12 | 13 |
| 14 | 15 | 16 | 17 | 18 | 19 | 20 |
| 21 | 22 | 23 | 24 | 25 | 26 | 27 |
| 28 | 29 | 30 | 31 | | | |

## August

| S | M | T | W | T | F | S |
|---|---|---|---|---|---|---|
| | | | | 1 | 2 | 3 |
| 4 | 5 | 6 | 7 | 8 | 9 | 10 |
| 11 | 12 | 13 | 14 | 15 | 16 | 17 |
| 18 | 19 | 20 | 21 | 22 | 23 | 24 |
| 25 | 26 | 27 | 28 | 29 | 30 | 31 |

## September

| S | M | T | W | T | F | S |
|---|---|---|---|---|---|---|
| 1 | 2 | 3 | 4 | 5 | 6 | 7 |
| 8 | 9 | 10 | 11 | 12 | 13 | 14 |
| 15 | 16 | 17 | 18 | 19 | 20 | 21 |
| 22 | 23 | 24 | 25 | 26 | 27 | 28 |
| 29 | 30 | | | | | |

## October

| S | M | T | W | T | F | S |
|---|---|---|---|---|---|---|
| | | 1 | 2 | 3 | 4 | 5 |
| 6 | 7 | 8 | 9 | 10 | 11 | 12 |
| 13 | 14 | 15 | 16 | 17 | 18 | 19 |
| 20 | 21 | 22 | 23 | 24 | 25 | 26 |
| 27 | 28 | 29 | 30 | 31 | | |

## November

| S | M | T | W | T | F | S |
|---|---|---|---|---|---|---|
| | | | | | 1 | 2 |
| 3 | 4 | 5 | 6 | 7 | 8 | 9 |
| 10 | 11 | 12 | 13 | 14 | 15 | 16 |
| 17 | 18 | 19 | 20 | 21 | 22 | 23 |
| 24 | 25 | 26 | 27 | 28 | 29 | 30 |

## December

| S | M | T | W | T | F | S |
|---|---|---|---|---|---|---|
| 1 | 2 | 3 | 4 | 5 | 6 | 7 |
| 8 | 9 | 10 | 11 | 12 | 13 | 14 |
| 15 | 16 | 17 | 18 | 19 | 20 | 21 |
| 22 | 23 | 24 | 25 | 26 | 27 | 28 |
| 29 | 30 | 31 | | | | |

# 2025

## January

| S | M | T | W | T | F | S |
|---|---|---|---|---|---|---|
|  |  |  | 1 | 2 | 3 | 4 |
| 5 | 6 | 7 | 8 | 9 | 10 | 11 |
| 12 | 13 | 14 | 15 | 16 | 17 | 18 |
| 19 | 20 | 21 | 22 | 23 | 24 | 25 |
| 26 | 27 | 28 | 29 | 30 | 31 |  |

## February

| S | M | T | W | T | F | S |
|---|---|---|---|---|---|---|
|  |  |  |  |  |  | 1 |
| 2 | 3 | 4 | 5 | 6 | 7 | 8 |
| 9 | 10 | 11 | 12 | 13 | 14 | 15 |
| 16 | 17 | 18 | 19 | 20 | 21 | 22 |
| 23 | 24 | 25 | 26 | 27 | 28 |  |

## March

| S | M | T | W | T | F | S |
|---|---|---|---|---|---|---|
|  |  |  |  |  |  | 1 |
| 2 | 3 | 4 | 5 | 6 | 7 | 8 |
| 9 | 10 | 11 | 12 | 13 | 14 | 15 |
| 16 | 17 | 18 | 19 | 20 | 21 | 22 |
| 23 | 24 | 25 | 26 | 27 | 28 | 29 |
| 30 | 31 |  |  |  |  |  |

## April

| S | M | T | W | T | F | S |
|---|---|---|---|---|---|---|
|  |  | 1 | 2 | 3 | 4 | 5 |
| 6 | 7 | 8 | 9 | 10 | 11 | 12 |
| 13 | 14 | 15 | 16 | 17 | 18 | 19 |
| 20 | 21 | 22 | 23 | 24 | 25 | 26 |
| 27 | 28 | 29 | 30 |  |  |  |

## May

| S | M | T | W | T | F | S |
|---|---|---|---|---|---|---|
|  |  |  |  | 1 | 2 | 3 |
| 4 | 5 | 6 | 7 | 8 | 9 | 10 |
| 11 | 12 | 13 | 14 | 15 | 16 | 17 |
| 18 | 19 | 20 | 21 | 22 | 23 | 24 |
| 25 | 26 | 27 | 28 | 29 | 30 | 31 |

## June

| S | M | T | W | T | F | S |
|---|---|---|---|---|---|---|
| 1 | 2 | 3 | 4 | 5 | 6 | 7 |
| 8 | 9 | 10 | 11 | 12 | 13 | 14 |
| 15 | 16 | 17 | 18 | 19 | 20 | 21 |
| 22 | 23 | 24 | 25 | 26 | 27 | 28 |
| 29 | 30 |  |  |  |  |  |

## July

| S | M | T | W | T | F | S |
|---|---|---|---|---|---|---|
|  |  | 1 | 2 | 3 | 4 | 5 |
| 6 | 7 | 8 | 9 | 10 | 11 | 12 |
| 13 | 14 | 15 | 16 | 17 | 18 | 19 |
| 20 | 21 | 22 | 23 | 24 | 25 | 26 |
| 27 | 28 | 29 | 30 | 31 |  |  |

## August

| S | M | T | W | T | F | S |
|---|---|---|---|---|---|---|
|  |  |  |  |  | 1 | 2 |
| 3 | 4 | 5 | 6 | 7 | 8 | 9 |
| 10 | 11 | 12 | 13 | 14 | 15 | 16 |
| 17 | 18 | 19 | 20 | 21 | 22 | 23 |
| 24 | 25 | 26 | 27 | 28 | 29 | 30 |
| 31 |  |  |  |  |  |  |

## September

| S | M | T | W | T | F | S |
|---|---|---|---|---|---|---|
|  | 1 | 2 | 3 | 4 | 5 | 6 |
| 7 | 8 | 9 | 10 | 11 | 12 | 13 |
| 14 | 15 | 16 | 17 | 18 | 19 | 20 |
| 21 | 22 | 23 | 24 | 25 | 26 | 27 |
| 28 | 29 | 30 |  |  |  |  |

## October

| S | M | T | W | T | F | S |
|---|---|---|---|---|---|---|
|  |  |  | 1 | 2 | 3 | 4 |
| 5 | 6 | 7 | 8 | 9 | 10 | 11 |
| 12 | 13 | 14 | 15 | 16 | 17 | 18 |
| 19 | 20 | 21 | 22 | 23 | 24 | 25 |
| 26 | 27 | 28 | 29 | 30 | 31 |  |

## November

| S | M | T | W | T | F | S |
|---|---|---|---|---|---|---|
|  |  |  |  |  |  | 1 |
| 2 | 3 | 4 | 5 | 6 | 7 | 8 |
| 9 | 10 | 11 | 12 | 13 | 14 | 15 |
| 16 | 17 | 18 | 19 | 20 | 21 | 22 |
| 23 | 24 | 25 | 26 | 27 | 28 | 29 |
| 30 |  |  |  |  |  |  |

## December

| S | M | T | W | T | F | S |
|---|---|---|---|---|---|---|
|  | 1 | 2 | 3 | 4 | 5 | 6 |
| 7 | 8 | 9 | 10 | 11 | 12 | 13 |
| 14 | 15 | 16 | 17 | 18 | 19 | 20 |
| 21 | 22 | 23 | 24 | 25 | 26 | 27 |
| 28 | 29 | 30 | 31 |  |  |  |

# 2024

# Daily Horoscope

Scorpio

*"Astrology is a Language. If you understand this language, The Sky Speaks to You."*
—Dane Rudhyar

# January

| Sun | Mon | Tue | Wed | Thu | Fri | Sat |
|-----|-----|-----|-----|-----|-----|-----|
|     | 1   | 2   | 3   | 4   | 5   | 6   |
| 7   | 8   | 9   | 10  | 11  | 12  | 13  |
| 14  | 15  | 16  | 17  | 18  | 19  | 20  |
| 21  | 22  | 23  | 24  | 25  | 26  | 27  |
| 28  | 29  | 30  | 31  |     |     |     |

# New Moon

# WOLF MOON

# JANUARY

**1 Monday**

You enter a time of transition that can feel unsettling; it brings memories as you revisit the past and contemplate treasured moments. You face a crossroads, but information emerges to connect you with others who bring support and fresh energy. Expanding your social life brings inspiration and news, which restores balance. An invitation to mingle initiates lively discussions and a sense of celebration that sparks fun moments.

**2 Tuesday**

The planet Mercury turns direct, and this positive cosmic change highlights expansion around your social life. An invitation arrives that brings a social aspect. It highlights heading out to gather with friends. It has you enjoying lively conversations that promote new ideas and rising creativity. Weaving a web of connectedness around your social life illustrates a rock-solid foundation. It encourages happiness and harmony as you deepen personal ties.

**3 Wednesday**

Being proactive and emphasizing improving circumstances helps you expand into new areas. It dissolves barriers and transitions to a journey that draws meaning and substance into your world. Instead of worrying about the destination, you get busy building foundations around your life that offer stability and progress. It lays the groundwork for the next leg of your journey through life. Research ahead helps design plans that light up areas of creativity, potential, and growth.

**4 Thursday**

The planet Mars sets up camp in Capricorn, and this planetary alignment creates a stable foundation to develop your work goals. Increasing drive attracts an ambitious focus to help you meet the challenges as you build your career path. Capricorn lends more security to the process of developing your goals. Your ability to manifest positive outcomes is increasing. It enables you to create tangible progress by developing a stable blueprint for future growth.

### 5 Friday

A carefree and happy chapter ahead brings fresh air and liberating times into your social life. Your river of hopes and dreams merges with inspiration, giving you a head start on developing your goals. You discover room to spread your wings, and sharing conversations sparks intriguing ideas worth your time. You enter an active and bustling phase of designing and growing life. News arrives that enables you to take tangible steps toward outlining strategies and building your dreams.

### 6 Saturday

You can expect developments around your social life to bring a fresh wave of possibility that offers excitement and joy. It lets you breathe fresh air into your surroundings as you feel renewed and embrace positive change. A new cycle begins, shifting your focus forward; it connects with others who offer thoughtful discussions. Sharing thoughts and ideas heightens the potential around your life and brings new possibilities into focus.

### 7 Sunday

A surprise invitation brings a radiant chapter that promotes growth in your circle of friends. Getting involved with creative enterprises and sharing with kindred spirits brings new adventures that have you feeling more connected with your cohort. Experimenting with developing new pathways attracts spice and excitement to keep life interesting. It lets you get busy crafting and designing plans for this year.

**8 Monday**

This week is a beautiful time to design and plan future growth opportunities. Imagination and creativity are rising, enabling you to access pathways that offer progress and growth. As you work towards your vision for growth, more structure and stability emerge. You benefit from expansion, and working with your abilities draws advancement. You hit the Jackpot and discover an enterprising time offering fortune and favor. Refining your gifts cracks the code to a bright chapter.

**9 Tuesday**

Mercury Square Neptune brings new insight into your life. Imagination rises, providing unique ideas and heightened problem-solving abilities. You are wise to stay open to change as a shift ahead brings a new foundation to your home and career life. It brings a unique chapter of growing your vision for future growth. Putting the finishing touches on your strategy enables you to generate the correct lead and head towards gold.

**10 Wednesday**

The Mars sextile Saturn aspect brings drive and energy to your daily tasks. Your powers of endurance heighten, enabling you to deal with all the activities on your plate and still have excess energy to burn. You land on solid ground as you build a robust basis from which to grow your talents. You benefit from developments on the horizon as it opens a busy time that nurtures a stable phase of growth and progression.

**11 Thursday**

Today, a New Moon offers the chance to plan goals and create a blueprint for future growth. News arrives that opens a new direction for your path. It brings a fresh cycle that helps you move towards more remarkable advancement. Deepening your knowledge and working with your abilities culminates in the kind of progress that takes your skills to the next level. A golden opportunity brings a pleasing result to your working life.

### 12 Friday

The Mars trine Jupiter aspect brings a boost to your spirits. It offers a favorable influence that puts the wind back in your sails. You are ready to attract greater abundance into your life. Releasing the past and creating space for new possibilities underscores your willingness to improve your circumstances. You scope out new prospects in an environment that offers an open road of potential. It emphasizes personal growth and sharing with the support of companions.

### 13 Saturday

Your social life picks up steam and opens a journey of adventure and excitement. It offers a curious change that brings improvement as it expands your circle of friends. You can expect developments around your social life to get a fresh wave of possibility that offers excitement and joy. It lets you breathe fresh air into your surroundings as you feel renewed and embrace positive change. A new cycle begins, shifting your focus forward.

### 14 Sunday

Mercury enters your $3^{rd}$ house of communication. This transit helps you express ideas to others and communicate thoughts freely and openly. Feelings evolve, and life becomes more connected when views are easily shared. An uptick of social invitations ahead brings fantastic potential into your life as you explore new pathways and get busy growing friendships with kindred spirits. Sharing thoughtful discussions replenishes emotional tanks and promotes happiness.

### 15 Monday

News arrives that brings new opportunities into your life. Being open to growing your world opens an active, lively, and productive chapter. New people come into your sphere to develop your talents and nurture thoughtful discussions which bring more abundance into your life. It offers a time of discovery as you plot a course toward a more connected environment shared with friends. Being open and sharing with others supports a lively and energetic chapter ahead.

### 16 Tuesday

The work you are doing will help you achieve a more secure landscape. Weeding out areas that do not serve your highest good help streamline your energy and direct your attention to the priorities that need your focus. Your courage and strength promote perseverance, enabling you to weather the storms and come out the other side and emerge under sunny skies. New opportunities ahead crack the code to a bright chapter.

### 17 Wednesday

You have a lot to share, and working with your talents will help you develop your abilities. Exploring leads brings a time of planning, designing, and investigation. It opens a path of vision and creativity when you stay open to learning new areas. Being resourceful and gathering your knowledge enables you to weave a basket of success. It takes you towards an environment ripe with blessings. An insightful person shares advice, bringing the potential for collaboration into focus.

### 18 Thursday

Getting involved in a group project brings the wind into your sails. It opens an engaging journey that offers rising prospects for your life. It brings a productive groove that nurtures creativity and cultivates advancement around your life. A unique aspect draws greater prosperity as you discover a path that brings new possibilities. It opens an expressive time of advancing your talents and working with your abilities to design and grow a passion project.

**19 Friday**

Venus faces Neptune in a square that encourages you to look at your romantic goals. You may be seeking something out of reach in your love life. Looking at the filters you have in your love life helps dispel myths and fantasies. Unfulfilled sexual desires may intertwine with unrealistic fanciful expectations and conspire to build an area of denial. This planetary aspect encourages you to take down the castles in the sky and plant your feet in terra firma.

**20 Saturday**

Today's Sun conjunct Pluto transit increases your power and ability to influence beneficial outcomes. Pluto sets up camp in Aquarius for the next 20 years. It brings the age of Pluto to Aquarius, a time of rising discoveries and scientific exploration. It will emphasize freedom-seeking and new ways of thinking, and this energy promotes developing creative approaches that heighten the potential. It is a welcome paradigm shift that offers to change the world.

**21 Sunday**

News arrives that hits a sweet note. It brings expansion to your social life. It does offer growth as you engage in a more connected environment that sweeps in fresh energy. It encourages you to walk the path that aligns with your heart's calling. An emphasis on developing personal bonds brings rising prospects for your love life. It offers companionship and brings abundance to your world. Thoughtful discussions get the ball rolling on improving emotional bonds.

## 22 Monday

You have been through a challenging time of rapid growth. It does place you in the proper alignment to grow your skills. A transition ahead brings heightened opportunities and aspirations aided by a flow of manifestation, bringing sunny skies overhead. You take on new assignments that showcase your abilities, which cracks the code to a successful outcome. Progress is soon within reach. Growing your world attracts happy moments that renew and restore your spirit.

## 23 Tuesday

Venus settles into Capricorn to heighten security in your life. It brings rising energy to your ambitions, helping fuel change in your life. It tempts you to develop creativity and nurture your skills. It places you in the proper alignment to grow life outwardly, cultivating rising prospects that help you make the most of your abilities in a progressive environment. It opens the gate to deepening your knowledge and elevating the options around your career.

## 24 Wednesday

The work you are doing will help you achieve a more secure landscape. Weeding out areas that do not serve your highest good help streamline your energy and direct your attention to the priorities that need your focus. Your courage and strength promote perseverance, enabling you to weather the storms and come out the other side and emerge under sunny skies. New opportunities ahead crack the code to a bright chapter.

## 25 Thursday

The Full Moon is a chance to unwind and turn inward as healing, and therapeutically helpful influences wash over your awareness. Being receptive to the Moon's healing qualities offers room to resolve any sensitive areas clinging to your spirit. Healing the past lays grounded foundations that secure rising possibilities in your social life. Taking time for reflection and healing lets you release any problematic emotions currently holding you back.

**26 Friday**

An invitation ahead brings a boost into your life as it provides an emphasis on improving social ties. It does get a chapter of fun and engagement that blends perfectly with your future hopes and dreams. You feel the influence of happiness beneath your wings, lifting you higher under sunny skies. You land in a productive and lively environment that enhances your social life. It brings a chance to network with others who provide a sense of collaboration and support.

**27 Saturday**

Today, the Sun square Jupiter aspect draws golden vibrations into your life. It raises confidence and leaves you feeling optimistic about your future potential. The curious changes ahead offer a compelling journey forward for your life. Indeed, it soon becomes a gateway from which to grow your world. You tap into a journey that brings a stimulating social environment that facilitates developing new areas.

**28 Sunday**

The Venus sextile Saturn transit today harmonizes personal bonds. It brings a levelheaded quality to your day-to-day interactions, promoting connection and balance. Lively conversations fuel expansion in your circle, bringing a trail of happiness to tempt you forward. Networking and mingling bring a happy way that bolsters your mood and improves the foundations around your life. It links you with a playful time that offers a bounty of engagement.

# FEBRUARY

| Sun | Mon | Tue | Wed | Thu | Fri | Sat |
|-----|-----|-----|-----|-----|-----|-----|
|     |     |     |     | 1   | 2   | 3   |
| 4   | 5   | 6   | 7   | 8   | 9   | 10  |
| 11  | 12  | 13  | 14  | 15  | 16  | 17  |
| 18  | 19  | 20  | 21  | 22  | 23  | 24  |
| 25  | 26  | 27  | 28  | 29  |     |     |

# NEW MOON

# SNOW MOON

**29 Monday**

Today's Venus trine Jupiter aspect draws beneficial outcomes into your social and personal life. Singles attract lively possibilities as they resonate with charm and magnetism. A lucky trine adds a dash of spontaneity to your life. You attract positive outcomes for your romantic life as changes arrive with a flourish to expand the borders. Thoughtful discussions bring romance and magic. It helps you explore developing romance in a lively and vibrant environment.

**30 Tuesday**

Life brims with unique possibilities that offer an active time of advancement. It brings an upgrade that captures the essence of dreams and potential. Opportunity comes knocking and opens your life to new flavors and possibilities. You reveal areas that tempt you to use your talents and work with your skills to advance life. It sees creativity blooming, and working with your abilities places you in the proper alignment to reach a golden avenue of possibility.

**31 Wednesday**

Harnessing the efficiency and effectiveness of your skills promotes advancement. It enables you to build stable foundations around your life. Getting involved in growing your skills unleashes your talents in an area that offers room to revolutionize your abilities. It brings an innovative and dynamic landscape that promotes creativity. It helps you establish your abilities in an avenue worth your time and attention. A chance for collaboration sparks interest and excitement.

**1 Thursday**

The good news ahead brings progression to the forefront of your life. It helps you achieve a goal you have been working towards and facilitates a new chapter that lets you quickly develop plans and grow your career path. Making your dreams a priority fast-tracks progression. It weeds out distractions and enables you to get busy developing life. Designing unique plans shapes an approach that represents the person you are becoming.

**2 Friday**

Today, intuition sparks under the Mercury sextile with Neptune. You may feel more sensitive under this cosmic influence. Still, it also increases communitive abilities, which helps you dig deeper and gain information below the surface of words and gestures. Lively discussions and in-depth communication deliver exciting possibilities. It translates to a time that builds your confidence and renews your spirit. It shines a light on a journey that glimmers with gold.

**3 Saturday**

An invitation to mingle promotes lively discussions and brings an open road of possibility. It draws harmony and abundance to your life as you get involved with growing companionship. It helps brew new opportunities by expanding your life and sharing time with kindred spirits. Indeed, plenty of unique happenings and invitations keep you optimistic about prospects. You discover a new joy in life, promoting a bustling and productive environment.

**4 Sunday**

Mercury ingress Aquarius has you seeking answers in your life; hot on the tail of this transit is Mercury conjunct Pluto, which adds intensity to personal communication. Probing questions reveal previously hidden answers. It helps you see your life from a unique perspective. It offers in-depth conversations that draw well-being into your world. Taking time to nurture and grow the path ahead brings a strong foundation.

**5 Monday**

A lot of incoming potential helps give you a leg up to growing your career path. It cracks the code to advance your abilities into a unique area that offers excellent prospects for your working life. It brings heightened growth and advancement into your life which secures a robust foundation from which to build the framework for inspiring goals as you get busy designing the plan ahead. It opens the path towards developing new possibilities for your life.

**6 Tuesday**

You head towards a unique landscape that nurtures growth and stability. Improving your bottom line heightens security and becomes a stable base to grow your life. Fortune shines brightly as expanding horizons attract new options. A purposeful push with a pioneering approach secures a fresh bounty of potential that brings lightness and momentum. A leap of faith into a new arena takes you on a beautiful journey of expanding horizons.

**7 Wednesday**

You find yourself flourishing in a new landscape of prosperity and happiness, surrounded by those who bring joy into your life and uplift your spirits. It signals a time of great abundance and growth as you move forward into a brighter future. It opens a new chapter filled with adventure and meaningful moments as you make new memories and deepen relationships that bring joy and happiness into your life.

**8 Thursday**

The Mars sextile with Neptune today raises charisma and increases your appeal to others. This planetary aspect improves confidence as you radiate charm and find social interactions easy and flowing. Choices and decisions shape fluid potential around your life, attracting a journey that weaves magic with a dash of transformation. Manifestation and intention work wonders in your world. You discover life soon moves from strength to strength.

**9 Friday**

Good fortune enters your life as you touch on a favorable chapter of possibility. Expect improvement in social areas as incoming news breathes fresh air into your social life. Getting involved with your social life draws benefits as you move towards an ample expressive, lively, and engaging time. You soon brew up a storm of possibility with treasured companions who inspire creative ideas and offer a chance to design projects worth developing.

**10 Saturday**

Mercury Square Jupiter adds distraction which brings a lapse of concentration. You may find it challenging to follow routines as your mind tends to wander under this planetary aspect. A lovely perk offers a soul-stirring time of thoughtful conversations. It helps you take advantage of elevated possibilities in your social life. Exploring new options fosters social engagement and brings a time of blending ideas and thoughts with others who nurture your creativity.

**11 Sunday**

You enter a busy and productive time for developing your romantic life. Moving away from outworn areas cracks the code to a brighter chapter in your love life. It opens a spotlight on nurturing dreams as you advance your situation towards growth. Sharing thoughtful discussions and companionship with someone who feels tailor-made for your life brings a happy chapter to your door. It seals the deal on a progressive time of developing romance.

**12 Monday**

You sink up with a lucky chapter that translates to an open road of potential for your love life. It carries news and information as you enter a time that draws sunshine and joy. You discover a personal bond that hums along, promoting a highly supportive and progressive connection. Sharing thoughts and kindling this situation lights a path that draws meaningful experiences and happiness. It does encourage romance in your life.

**13 Tuesday**

Mars ingress Aquarius brings forward-thinking ideas that revolutionize the potential possible in your world. The Venus sextile Neptune brings a sense of anticipation into your life that has you looking forward to Valentine's Day. It offers big-sky dreaming as you indulge in romantic fantasies. Listening to the music within your heart attracts an expressive and heartfelt journey as you align with destiny.

**14 Wednesday**

Mars conjunct Pluto brings the drive and passion to your goals. It heightens sexual drive and desires, helping you nail your romantic goals today. Making your life a priority hits a sweet note that opens a path toward developing romance. Thoughtful discussions bring sunshine and light to your surroundings, bringing ideal conditions to grow a bond that feels suitable for your life. It offers a wellspring of happiness for your romantic life.

**15 Thursday**

You soon reveal a touch of magic that arrives to bless your life with a more social environment. Opportunities to mingle lift the lid on a curious time of expanding your circle of friends. Harnessing the possibilities available in your life lets you explore options that offer a golden phase of rising potential. Being open and sharing with others supports a lively and energetic chapter. It brings invitations that expand the borders and helps you achieve growth.

**16 Friday**

Venus sashays into Aquarius to raise the vibration in your romantic life. It showers harmonious beams over your social world, contributing to rising prospects in your life. It brings growth to your love life and lights up pathways of connectedness and companionship. It brings a breakthrough of lively interactions and thoughtful discussions. As you plug into a journey that aligns with destiny, you feel more in tune with the path forward for your world.

**17 Saturday**

Being open to new possibilities brings excitement as you discover a journey that speaks to your heart. It rules a time of advancing life towards rising prospects. It offers a social aspect that brings connection and support. Meaningful gestures set the tone for developing stable foundations which promote a better sense of harmony in your world. It offers lighter energy that anchors you to a grounded and secure environment that promotes happiness.

**18 Sunday**

You unlock the gate to a bright time that offers many blessings. It brings stability and balance into your home life, creating solid foundations to grow your world. Designing plans brings a buzz of excitement as you feel creatively inspired. It helps you remove limiting beliefs and embark on a journey that offers advancement. It gets an upgrade to your home life that opens a path toward growth. Life becomes more manageable as you discover a journey of ease and plenty.

**19 Monday**

Today brings a lighter time that sees the goodness flowing as you enjoy expansion in your social life. Connecting with other creative people draws support and gives a time of sharing companionship to your door. You attract a rich and abundant landscape that encourages social engagement and encourages invitations to mingle. Your social life is ripening, bringing unique options that open a path forward. A ray of sunshine puts a spring in your step as you ease into new routines.

**20 Tuesday**

You soon break fresh ground as new options come knocking to get you thinking about the possibilities. Being proactive and developing your talents brings rising prospects that link with a trajectory offering growth and progress. You discover a different landscape that benefits you from greater harmony. Your willingness to be open to change provides substantial benefits. A situation you invest energy into developing grows wings and takes flight along with your dreams.

**21 Wednesday**

News arrives that brings a boost and leaves you feeling optimistic about growing options that open the door to attractively developing your life. Nurturing talents brings ample time for cultivating advancement. It charts a course towards setting goals that promote your abilities and grow your skills. It generates a time of lively discussions shared with others who resonate on your wavelength. It gives you the green light to move forward toward designing goals.

**22 Thursday**

Venus conjunct Mars increases sexual charisma and drive. It heightens intimacy and yearning for exceptional bonding. If you crave romantic downtime today, you know which planets are involved in the passion propelling you toward creating magic and mayhem in your love life. A buzz of activity ahead attracts romance and thoughtful discussions. Meaningful gestures set the tone for developing stable foundations which promote a better sense of connection in your world.

**23 Friday**

Thanks to Mercury slipping into Pisces to increase your thought processes, you receive a boost of mental clarity and an uptick in analytical reasoning abilities today. It opens a productive environment that lets you carve out a journey that offers progression. You lift the shutters with an enterprising position that takes your talents further as you advance life onward. Good news ahead brings optimism and excitement, as it is the fresh start you have been seeking.

**24 Saturday**

A Full moon in Virgo draws understanding, clarity, and insight. It offers a broader overview of your life, nurturing a therapeutic and healing environment. There is healing and releasing, which wipes the slate clean. You can harness the energy of forgiveness is a powerful tool to improve bonds and draw balance into your life. You open a journey that draws transformation and happiness as it replenishes emotional tanks. You attract enriching possibilities that release the heaviness.

**25 Sunday**

Venus Square Jupiter's planetary aspect brings a fun-loving vibe into your social life. Good fortune, sharing, and caring with friends light an engaging path that nurtures well-being and happiness in your life. A little worn avenue opens and brings good luck and happiness. Something percolating in the background makes a grand arrival with a splash of color. It invites you to connect with friends and broaden your life with opportunities to expand your circle.

**26 Monday**

Many changes in your life help improve your bottom line. You make notable tracks on learning a new area that lifts the lid on rising prospects. Taking your abilities towards advancement draws an optimistic journey that sees life pick up the pace. It connects you with others who offer help, bringing growth and expansion to your circle of friends. It helps you breeze through to an active phase of designing new goals.

**27 Tuesday**

Mars square Jupiter brings positive energy, heightening confidence and enthusiasm for life. You enter a busy time in your career, which enables you to create pivotal change and head toward advancement. An upgrade ahead brings a prosperous cycle that directs your energy toward developing your skills. You migrate away from troubles and enjoy a bright and breezy aspect that builds a life path with creativity, flexibility, and innovation.

**28 Wednesday**

Sun conjunct Mercury brings news and communication. Your hard work and contributions are valued and appreciated. You receive notification of a promotion or windfall opportunity that advances life to a new growth cycle. Information ahead helps you create progress in developing your skills. It brings a blossoming time of activity that transitions you to an area worth your time. You soon get busy designing new projects that enable advancement to keep your inspiration firing.

**29 Thursday**

Jupiter's positive vibration seals that deal on a Mercury-infused forward-thinking day. Mercury in sextile with Jupiter offers an ideal opportunity to think about the future and brainstorm as you plan future goals. Going after your dreams and exploring leads draws a positive result. When you advance your talents, you tune into a broader possible landscape. A whirlwind of new options helps you establish a progressive foundation around your career path.

# MARCH

| Sun | Mon | Tue | Wed | Thu | Fri | Sat |
|-----|-----|-----|-----|-----|-----|-----|
|     |     |     |     |     | 1   | 2   |
| 3   | 4   | 5   | 6   | 7   | 8   | 9   |
| 10  | 11  | 12  | 13  | 14  | 15  | 16  |
| 17  | 18  | 19  | 20  | 21  | 22  | 23  |
| 24  | 25  | 26  | 27  | 28  | 29  | 30  |
| 31  |     |     |     |     |     |     |

# SCORPIO

# New Moon

# WORM MOON

_____

_____

_____

_____

_____

_____

_____

_____

_____

_____

_____

_____

_____

_____

_____

_____

_____

_____

_____

_____

_____

# MARCH

### 1 Friday

One of astrology's most favored transits lights up your day. In sextile with Jupiter, the Sun brings golden beams of positivity into your life. Curious possibilities ahead light a positive aspect that enables you to capitalize on this new potential. Directing your energy towards developing leads brings a vital journey that promotes greater prosperity and happiness. You enter a busy time of substance, progress, and reward. Working towards your vision enables a pleasing outcome.

### 2 Saturday

News arrives, which lights a journey of expansion. You open a windfall opportunity that gets the ball rolling on developing unique areas which hold meaning. You connect with like-minded people who offer creative insights and practical solutions. Getting involved with your broader community environment brings wellness and happiness to the forefront of your world. It engenders positive feelings as you enjoy a more connected environment around your social life.

### 3 Sunday

Venus Square Uranus brings restless energy that offers deliberate you from constraints that keep you tied down and feeling limited. You feel called to liberate yourself from restrictive circumstances and patterns. It brings a spontaneous element that promotes refreshing adventures that change your day-to-day routines. Changes ahead improve the building blocks of your life. Directing your attention to your social life brings a rewarding journey that promotes happiness.

### 4 Monday

Researching options and planning for future growth helps you move forward with conviction with a correct approach. You trigger a journey of expanding opportunities by being open to progressing your skills and developing your talents. Designing the way ahead offers a bright and optimistic fresh start. Good news arrives with excitement and opens a positive trend in your life. It is a surprise that carries a bonus that boosts your mood and emphasizes expansion.

### 5 Tuesday

You lean into challenges and embrace growing your abilities. Working with your talents helps you close the door on a difficult time, and as the chaos fades, you discover a lucky aspect that draws good fortune. You become involved in using your talents to design and grow a path forward. Creating space to nurture abilities brings a unique landscape that promotes creativity. Developments ahead allow pieces of the puzzle to fall into place, creating a bigger picture.

### 6 Wednesday

Putting your talents center stage elevates potential and sparks increasing options that promote security. It encourages expansion and culminates in an upgrade to your situation. An emphasis on designing goals brings exciting plans ahead. It is a time that carries you towards a lighter foundation. It does bring positive possibilities that have a substantial impact on improving the journey ahead in your life.

### 7 Thursday

New options ahead help you turn the corner and enter a time of rising possibilities. Focusing on improving life becomes an emphasis that promotes greater security and happiness. It opens a refreshing chapter that rules imagination, creativity, and innovation. Being open to change lets you break free from restrictive patterns that currently hold life back. Events align to nourish your world with new options that point the way forward for your life.

**8 Friday**

A new page opens in your book of life when you enter a fantastic time for connecting with your circle of friends. It opens a time of sharing thoughts and discussions that take you towards a winning environment. It cultivates a surge of positive energy that brings progress and expansion as you open life to a new flavor. Life turns full circle as you lift the lid on an enterprising chapter that brings exciting developments into your social life.

**9 Saturday**

A Mars square Uranus planetary transit hits a freedom-loving vibe in time for Saturday night adventures. It brings a restlessness that seeks expression as you break free from constraints and head towards a liberating time shared with friends. New possibilities ahead kick off a time of sunshine and sparkle, which brings celebration into your life. It promotes stimulating conversations in a social environment that feel good for your soul.

**10 Sunday**

Mercury ingress Aries offers improvement as newfound energy and drive help you accomplish a great deal. It is a time that carries you towards a lighter foundation. It does bring positive possibilities that have a substantial impact on improving the journey ahead in your life. Developing your goals and designing projects that inspire and delight help you put the finishing touches on your plans. Improvement overhead marks an essential new beginning that ushers in fresh possibilities.

### 11 Monday

Venus ingress Pisces is a favorable transit for your love life. It harmonizes emotional bonds and elevates potential in your personal life. New possibilities draw companionship, and this promotes enrichment and social involvement. Magic and creativity weave a prosperous path toward an exciting landscape of opportunity. You enter a busy time that removes the blocks that stall progress as news arrives to flick the switch on an engaging chapter for expansion.

### 12 Tuesday

A focus on self-development draws an abundant landscape. It brings transformation that sees sunnier skies emerging overhead. As you open to the possibilities that flow into your life, you align with your core values as you grow your abilities and nurture stable foundations. Serendipitous changes ahead give you glimmers of possibility, and following this trial draws prosperity. It enables you to craft a blossoming path as you design goals that suit your expertise.

### 13 Wednesday

A path opens off the beaten track. Being resourceful offers practical solutions and a chance to grow a journey that offers advancement. As you deepen your knowledge and expand your skills, it opens to a productive environment where you can gain traction in developing your vision for future growth. Exploring options around your life brings an empowering sense of confidence which helps shape new goals.

### 14 Thursday

Notable changes ahead transform life into a busy time. It brings an approach that offers positivity as you mark a turning point and expand life outwardly. Exploring leads jumpstarts growth and helps you push back the barriers to achieve a successful outcome. Unique prospects ahead offer golden returns on your time. As momentum gathers, you discover an upgrade that brings excitement and joy. News arrives that gives you a brighter picture of the path ahead.

### 15 Friday

News arrives, which opens growth pathways in your social life. It helps you blaze a happy trail toward a more connected future. You attend a social gathering with lights, music, and dancing. It brings lively discussions and insightful possibilities which inspire expansion in your world. It brings invitations to circulate with friends, which expands the borders and brings new people into your sphere. It leaves you feeling refreshed and ready to take on the world.

### 16 Saturday

Fortune aligns to get a new source of happiness into your world. It lets you chart a course toward a stable and supportive landscape that offers expansion. It draws a busy time of engaging with your circle of friends. A wellspring of magic and opportunities to mingle course through your social life, improving valuable bonds. This wave of social engagement offers a happy time shared with friends, which inspires positivity and joy.

### 17 Sunday

Sun conjunct Neptune transit increases intuition and empathy today. It brings an appropriate time to reflect and contemplate future dreams and goals. It begins an enriching journey that draws a productive, active pace and sets the tone for growing life and using your talents significantly. New possibilities emerge, bringing a sound platform to deepen your knowledge and advance your skills. You enter a goal-orientated phase of designing strategic plans and expanding life.

**18 Monday**

A new area ahead brings rising prospects as you take on a winning trajectory that offers an upgrade for your life. It brings an essential time of growth that offers increasing possibilities as you begin to see what is achievable when you tap into hidden strengths and grow your abilities. It opens an exciting time of working with your skills and deepening your knowledge to crack the code to a bright chapter in your working life.

**19 Tuesday**

A richer landscape of possibility reawakens your senses to the potential around your world when you engage with opportunities to grow. New projects and endeavors bring the spark into your life, offering an upgrade. You take your talents into uncharted territory and upscale your skills, bringing curious options to light. It draws a busy and productive time for developing goals and working with your abilities. You hone in on rising potential that takes your gifts to a new level.

**20 Wednesday**

Exploring leads and pulling out all the stops to achieve your chosen destination helps you build rising prospects as you open to unique possibilities that offer advancement. You extend your reach into an area that grows your skills. It opens a positive trend that takes your abilities to the next level. Rising prospects on the horizon ensure a pleasing result ahead. It draws an enterprising time that brightens your life with possibility.

**21 Thursday**

Sun sextile Pluto transit increases your drive. You feel more determined and purposeful than usual, which helps you achieve your goals today. It lets you progress and expand your horizons into areas that deepen your knowledge and grow your abilities. New possibilities raise confidence and bring a newfound energy to develop projects of meaning. It ignites a passion for working with your skills and increasing life outwardly.

**22 Friday**

The transit of Mars in Pisces reduces issues in your life as this favorable aspect draws good fortune and rising prospects. It elevates financial possibilities, leading to a winning path forward. You spotlight an avenue that provides fruitful results. It shines a light on a productive phase of growth that promotes a strong basis of grounded foundations. Choices and decisions ahead take you towards a lofty destination.

**23 Saturday**

New horizons grow and expand your social life, bringing a bustling environment and invitations to share with others who hold meaning in your world. Optimism and inspiration figure prominently during this lively time. Good fortune is rising as you unpack a journey brimming with possibility. It brings a social aspect that promotes invitations and opportunities to mingle. It helps you break fresh ground as you expand your circle of friends.

**24 Sunday**

Venus sextile Jupiter raises confidence as good fortune flows into your life. It introduces a lucky aspect that improves finances, relationships, and circumstances. A window of opportunity opens and brings valuable rewards on offer. Life heads on an upswing and offers a new source of prosperity. Good fortune secures a pleasing result which builds greater happiness in your life. It promotes sound foundations that nurture your home and family life.

### 25 Monday

A Full Moon brings healing into your surroundings to wash away the outworn areas and soothe your spirit with a therapeutic influence. Taking time for reflection and healing creates space to nurture well-being and happiness. It lets you release any problematic emotions that are currently holding you back. A healing influence surrounds your situation, enabling you to draw rejuvenation into the roots of your being.

### 26 Tuesday

Creativity heightens, allowing you to develop creative expression and embark on a phase of personal growth. Taking a step back gives you a broader overview of what is possible when you think outside the box—expanding the scope of your search rings in curious possibilities tinged in gold. Prospects brighten, bringing a rock-solid foundation from which to grow your life. It advances your abilities and cultivates rising opportunities.

### 27 Wednesday

Exploring opportunities in your broader community brings a nurturing influence that promotes joy and warmth. It shines a light on expanding connections as you broaden your horizons and grow bonds around your social life. The path ahead clears as communication arrives, bringing positive energy into your life. It links you with kindred spirits, and increasing social options nourish your soul with thoughtful discussions.

### 28 Thursday

A fresh start ahead brings rising prospects into your life. It marks a journey that is adventurous, social, and expansive. It brings opportunities to mingle and connect with your broader circle of friends. Sharing companionship and communication replenishes emotional tanks and provides a meaningful aspect that promotes harmony. It lays the groundwork for developing your social bonds. A happy time ahead brings grounded and secure foundations.

### 29 Friday

You receive an invitation that lets your social life head on an upswing. As you light up pathways of connectedness and social engagement, you open the gate to refreshing possibilities that draw lighter energy into your life. You enter a cycle of increasing happiness that brings radiance your way. News worth celebrating lands on your doorstep, putting you in a mood to mingle with friends and enjoy companionship.

### 30 Saturday

Adventure comes calling and links you to a social environment. You receive an invitation that captures the essence of wanderlust and adventure. An expressive and trailblazing time of sharing thoughtful discussions begins a positive trend that expands your social life outwardly. It unleashes a lively environment that brings a chance to mingle with friends. Nurturing personal bonds promotes happiness and well-being.

### 31 Sunday

This Easter, you may notice a sentimental vibe that brings a softness into your life. Poetic and insightful energy creates a cocoon around your soul. Devoting time to dabbling in your hobbies and connecting with friends and family sees you feel content and secure. Focusing on priorities brings happiness and harmony to your door. You settle into a happy time filled with warmth and joy as it links you with others who offer a supportive and group environment.

# APRIL

| Sun | Mon | Tue | Wed | Thu | Fri | Sat |
|-----|-----|-----|-----|-----|-----|-----|
|     | 1   | 2   | 3   | 4   | 5   | 6   |
| 7   | 8   | 9   | 10  | 11  | 12  | 13  |
| 14  | 15  | 16  | 17  | 18  | 19  | 20  |
| 21  | 22  | 23  | 24  | 25  | 26  | 27  |
| 28  | 29  | 30  |     |     |     |     |

# NEW MOON

## Pink Moon

# APRIL

## 1 Monday

Mercury turns Retrograde on April Fools' Day, bringing a little joke from the heavens. It is a time that stalls progress as miscommunication and mixed signals are more prevalent in your social life. It governs a slower phase that helps you turn away from areas that no longer inspire or motivate your spirit. As you step away from drama and maintain mindfulness that miscommunication and challenging crosscurrents can impede progress, it helps you adeptly manage this transit.

## 2 Tuesday

Events on the horizon encourage you to nourish your world with genuine opportunities that bring happiness. Further information opens a landscape ripe with possibility, and reshaping goals helps bring a burst of sunshine into your world as you discover a little worn path opens and offers to revolutionize the potential possible in your situation. An opportunity that feels like the right fit for your life pops up. It initiates a time of rapid progress and rising prospects.

## 3 Wednesday

Venus conjunct Neptune brings rising possibilities for singles to find a romantic partner. It also offers advancement for couples as a favorable influence nurtures growth. A spotlight on expanding your life highlights a time of social engagement, stimulating activities, and entertaining dialogues. It offers a supportive journey that brings new possibilities into your life. It may even get a chance to deepen a bond that inspires harmony and romance.

## 4 Thursday

News arrives that helps you touch down on new potential. It takes your dreams to the next level as you become more proactive about designing unique goals which serve your creativity well. It does bring learning, growth, and improvement as you develop an endeavor that offers advancement. It does open a productive time of growing the potential around your life. It is a fruitful time to get busy and focus on building stability as growth is ahead.

## 5 Friday

Venus ingress Aries brings a thoughtful aspect that helps you rediscover your passion and creativity. It places the spotlight on nurturing hobbies and growing interests in your life. A fresh cycle beckons and enables you to move toward new possibilities. It gives you the green light to cultivate change by working with your creativity and nurturing your talents. Clear skies breeze into your life, bringing curious options to explore.

## 6 Saturday

Venus sextile Pluto adds depth, meaning, and curiosity. It has you wanting to peel back the layers and discover what lies beneath the surface of everyday life. It awakens creative inspiration that becomes the gateway from which you develop unique goals which hold meaning. Nurturing your dreams stirs the energy of manifestation that increases creativity and helps you discover a journey that is the essence of inspiration. The seeds you plant revolutionize and transform your life.

## 7 Sunday

Unexpected news materializes and brings a journey filled with promise. It unlocks the key to tremendous success and optimism in your life. You discover heartwarming progress around your social life that gets a boost that offers unique possibilities. Sharing ideas and thoughts with friends helps you uncover individual information that promotes support and guidance in your world. Life attracts an array of opportunities that bring new options to your table.

**8 Monday**

An opportunity ahead helps you create headway around developing a big goal. It encourages you to dream big, gives energy, and drives you to establish the path. It culminates in a shift that has you building new foundations that feel like the right direction for your life. News arrives that banishes clouds and brings sunny skies overhead. It helps you spread your wings and take flight toward designing a vision for future growth.

**9 Tuesday**

You find you can pivot away from areas that limit progress and head towards advancement. It anchors your energy in a productive environment that draws grounded foundations as you create space to develop your goals. Working with your talents helps create a stimulating and progressive environment. Opportunities ahead improve the security in your working life. It brings rising prospects that help you gain traction on advancing your career.

**10 Wednesday**

Mars conjunct Saturn ignites determination and drive, which helps you excel in the workplace. Expanding your life into unique areas offers a positive shift that attracts possibilities worth your time. Designing your life draws progression and aligns you toward achieving a positive result. A new attitude and rising confidence bring a chance to step out and enjoy growing a path that offers room to revolutionize the potential possible in your world.

**11 Thursday**

The winds of change breathe fresh energy into your spirit; it enables you to progress life towards an exciting area. It attracts and promotes renewal which cleans the slate and places you in prime alignment to expand life outwardly when news arrives which captures your interest. There is much to look forward to as it marks the start of a refreshing chapter of social engagement in your life. Curious information comes that brings lively discussions shared with friends.

**12 Friday**

You are heading towards a socially busy time that brings a boost of lighter energy into your life. Invitations to mingle keep life bubbling along with possibility. It opens a sweet time of communication that lights a journey of friendship and engagement. You step into a lively chapter that nurtures harmony in your life. It triggers options that draw happiness as you get busy sharing with friends. You unlock the key to an essential time of growing your life in a unique direction.

**13 Saturday**

News arrives that secures an invitation to mingle. It helps you turn a corner and enter a light chapter of companionship and growing social opportunities. You enter a busy time brimming with opportunities to network and connect with your social circle. Serendipity paves the way forward, promoting kinship with someone who offers thoughtful gestures and lively discussions. You soon seal the deal on growing life outwardly.

**14 Sunday**

You enter a bright time that improves security and balance around the foundations of your home. It helps you reawaken to the rich landscape of possibility in your life, and this removes the blocks as it gets you in contact with others who help drive your energy forward with the essence of creative inspiration. It fuels a connected environment that sees you working with your talents and mingling with others.

### 15 Monday

Opening life to new pathways takes you towards unprecedented growth and rising prospects. The more you become involved in developing your knowledge and deepening your abilities, the more opportunities come to meet you on the road to success. You are on a continuous cycle of evolution, growth, and change. Beneficial changes let you glimpse a glimmering path forward that brings lighter energy your way.

### 16 Tuesday

Leaning into the challenges ahead grows your talents and takes your skills to the next level. It unlocks essential information that helps you move away from areas that derail progress as you turn the corner and head toward growth. You harness the energy of courage and drive to make the most of extending your talents into a new area worth your time. In-depth research and insightful discussions help you develop projects that expand your life.

### 17 Wednesday

Your situation is changing and evolving, bringing rising possibilities that encourage expansion. Exploring leads helps you unearth the right direction for your life as you unearth a purposeful and optimistic avenue ready to develop. It gives you the green light to move forward toward growing your life. Nurturing your abilities and progressing forward enables you to plot a course toward more lofty goals.

### 18 Thursday

Opportunities ahead create a greater sense of security and ease in your life. A focus on improving circumstances brings stability and balance to your door. It helps you ride out any turbulence and find the inspiration to embark on growth goals. A re-evaluation is a helpful tool as it streamlines and elevates the potential around your life. New options improve your working life and open a way of growth for your career path.

### 19 Friday

Mars sextile Jupiter transit makes you feel confident today. This planetary aspect is ideal for tackling complex tasks because there is an excellent chance of success. This transit has a well-earned reputation for good luck as it increases optimism and initiative and brings a willingness to take calculated risks. Developing your goals helps improve the priorities in your life. Understanding the broader picture of options surrounding your life cracks the code for a well-designed journey.

### 20 Saturday

Mars sextile Uranus offers unique ideas that help you think outside the box to obtain innovative solutions. Uranus places the focus on rebellion, liberation, and freedom. It adds a dash of spontaneity to your life today. You head towards an active time of engaging with your social life. It brings outings and opportunities that feel adventurous. Keeping life vivid and dynamic draws happy times that uplift the mood. You find flavor by adding variety to your life.

### 21 Sunday

Jupiter's conjunct Uranus transit provides surprises and sudden opportunities. Good news lands in a flurry of excitement. It brings the music into your surroundings as thoughtful conversations draw happiness. It opens a perfect time to step out into a community environment and engage with others who support your life. It opens a self-expressive, joyful, and happy time spent with kindred spirits.

**22 Monday**

This week becomes a source of inspiration as life greets you with new possibilities that take your skills to the next level. Focusing on developing your life helps put your unique touch on curious goals that mark improvement in your life. It brings an approach that captures the essence of inspiration as you soon ignite the fires of creativity within your belly. Developing your vision for future growth enables you to take advantage of building options that offer room to progress your skills.

**23 Tuesday**

The Full Moon draws a healing and therapeutic influence into your life. You are in a time of transition that can feel unsettling as sensitive emotions rise to be released. It attracts a healing effect that reverberates around your life, enabling you to make peace with the past and understand what has gone before is all part of your life's journey. Distancing drama and rebooting your life create foundations that harmonize and enrich your world.

**24 Wednesday**

Your fortune is heading towards a rising aspect. It brings enterprising avenues which develop your talents and refine your abilities. Working with your skills brings the chance to build the path forward for your career. An ever-widening circle of possibilities reverberates around your situation, enabling you to head toward a successful outcome. You enter a busy time that brings refinement, progression, and advancement.

**25 Thursday**

Mercury turns direct, improving personal bonds and opening the path to growing your social life. Lovely changes nurture a lively and inspiring course ahead. It creates space for grounded foundations that draw peace and stability. As you mingle and network with your broader circle, you discover insight into the path ahead. Sharing with friends and family creates a sound foundation that restocks and refuels your spirit.

**26 Friday**

Making yourself a priority puts specific goals front and center as you expand your world and connect with others who radiate your wavelength. It begins a journey that feels right for your soul as it brings new people into your life who help you live life to the fullest. Your creativity is a valuable tool to help you forge a unique path in your life. You score a win when news arrives, which inspires growth. It brings a chance to reinvent yourself in a new area.

**27 Saturday**

A time of transformation heats a lighter chapter that offers social engagement and community involvement. It launches a time of promoting stable foundations as you get busy with new projects on the home front. Building sound foundations ushers a fruitful time to link with your circle of friends. It emphasizes improving the home and family life as you mix with friends who offer companionship. It culminates in a happy time that offers rising prospects for your life.

**28 Sunday**

More stability emerges around your home life. It does bring a surge of inspiration that enables you to gain a better environment in your world. You enter a time of transformation that promotes positive change ahead. It helps deliver good news and bring rising prospects into your home and family life. It brings a time of sharing abundance and growing your world outwardly. Surrounding yourself with good energy creates an abundant landscape of possibility that nurtures your spirit.

# MAY

| Sun | Mon | Tue | Wed | Thu | Fri | Sat |
|-----|-----|-----|-----|-----|-----|-----|
|     |     |     | 1   | 2   | 3   | 4   |
| 5   | 6   | 7   | 8   | 9   | 10  | 11  |
| 12  | 13  | 14  | 15  | 16  | 17  | 18  |
| 19  | 20  | 21  | 22  | 23  | 24  | 25  |
| 26  | 27  | 28  | 29  | 30  | 31  |     |

# New Moon

# FLOWER MOON

**29 Monday**

Venus in Taurus brings a harmonizing influence that offers grounded foundations for your social life. It helps you approach relationships and life warmly, earthy and balanced manner. Today, a Mars conjunct Neptune aspect raises potential in your romantic life; it has you dreaming big about the possibilities. Engaging in lively conversation, you reveal there is plenty to celebrate. It infuses your life with new prospects by discussing ideas and sharing thoughts with a kindred spirit.

**30 Tuesday**

Mars lands in Aries, and this raises confidence. It's time to go big and be bold. Your best qualities will enter the spotlight and gain recognition soon. It brings a page-turning chapter when the path ahead clears. You enter a busy time that carries news and information your way. It opens a social landscape that lets you kick up your heels and enjoy sharing with friends. Connecting with your broader circle of friends offers companionship that hits a sweet note.

**1 Wednesday**

A social opportunity helps you break free from constraints and enjoy a liberating time shared with friends. However, today's aspect could see a flare-up of jealousy or possessiveness. Your romantic partner may feel threatened by heightened social activities and invitations flowing into your life. Take time to support and boost confidence to help offset the Venus square Pluto aspect. Being aware of these fears' dynamics helps keep relationships healthy and balanced.

**2 Thursday**

Pluto is the modern ruler of Scorpio; it symbolizes how we experience power, renewal, rebirth, and mysterious or subconscious forces. This Pluto retrograde phase allows you to dive deep and explore inner realms and darker aspects of your personality ordinarily hidden from view. Understanding your psyche deeper provides access to the forces driving your personality. Changes ahead stir the pot of manifestation and offer an enriching brew for your life.

### 3 Friday

Mars sextile Pluto transit increases energy in the workplace. No job is too small as you take on the lot and work towards your vision. Working effectively and efficiently towards your goals hold you in good stead. You no longer feel as though you are treading water; you begin to see the progress you have worked tirelessly to achieve. It places you in the correct alignment to advance as you get busy working with your abilities to bring the cream to the top of your life.

### 4 Saturday

News arrives, which enables you to plot a course toward greater security in your life. It brings improvement to your home and living situation. An upbeat vibe works wonders for your self-esteem and confidence. It brings a social aspect that sees you spending more time with friends and kindred spirits. Enjoyable moments blossom, drawing happiness and expansion. Sharing with others gets a boost, and as morale rises, you discover new pathways tempting you forward.

### 5 Sunday

Actively tapping into the potential around your creativity attracts a new assignment worth your time. Opportunities ahead offer changes to your home life. A busy time of developing goals draws a whirlwind of liberty that has you dreaming big about the potential. Creativity rises, bringing movement and progress to your social life as you unpack a lively chapter shared with kindred spirits who brighten your life.

### 6 Monday

Positive feedback arrives to boost your spirit. It shines a light on a path that promotes your goals and dreams. Ambitious stirrings bring life to new projects and endeavors. Working with your skills enables a pleasing result and aligns you with more outstanding options for your career path. The climate around your life ripens and opens attractive avenues which offer growth and progress. It all helps upgrade your life to the next level.

### 7 Tuesday

Sun sextile Saturn transit lends patience and perseverance; it enables you to gain traction on achieving challenging goals in your life. Creating space to nurture abilities brings a unique landscape that promotes creativity. You discover a pathway that captures the essence of inspiration as your imagination dreams up refreshing possibilities that become a source of happiness as you attract positive results. It progresses skills and elevates prospects around your career.

### 8 Wednesday

You head toward growth and advancement. Being proactive helps you create gateways that promote your talents. It triggers a path that offers advanced options to grow your working life. You soon feel things are improving as you deepen your knowledge and advance your abilities in new areas. It initiates a time of growth and evolution that promotes a successful outcome in your working life. It ignites a passion for working with your skills and increasing your life outwardly.

### 9 Thursday

The path ahead clears, bringing a succession of positive outcomes that have you feeling optimistic about your career life. Focusing on the building blocks and setting your intentions enables you to make the most of the changes ahead. As you deepen your knowledge and advance your skills, you extend your reach into new areas worth your time. A new phase soon cranks up the level of growth in your career.

**10 Friday**

Confidence is growing as you connect with options that inspire growth. It brings a time of embracing fun, connection, and kinship. Lively conversations draw an engaging chapter of networking with friends in a relaxed environment. With invitations and possibilities, life picks up, which promotes growing friendships. Supportive energy hits the ticket for a robust environment as increasing choices add a sweet flavor that prepares you for new adventures shared with friends.

**11 Saturday**

Life is ready to beam new opportunities into your world. It brings a busy time filled with exciting developments that enable you to create progress. You discover focusing on developing your social life attracts a rewarding outcome. Clear skies breeze into your social life, bringing insightful discussions as emotional well-being soars to new heights. As you make notable tracks on developing goals, freedom and expansion come calling to expand horizons.

**12 Sunday**

You can make your dreams a priority as you enter a phase of fresh starts that build grounded foundations around your world. An emphasis on your home situation sees life move forward toward greener pastures. You open a journey of rising prospects that sees a theme of greater abundance emerging in your life. It seals the deal on developing goals and nurturing your dreams as you set the bar higher around your life.

## 13 Monday

A positive influence from the Sun conjunct Uranus planetary aspect brings a boost that sparks new options. The Venus sextile Saturn transit today increases your need for company, and you may yearn to connect with friends. An invitation arrives that enables you to turn a corner and head towards a brighter and lighter phase of developing social bonds. It brings an engaging time that offers new possibilities and pathways.

## 14 Tuesday

A new journey is approaching for your life. The timing is fortunate as you connect with friends who nurture your world's foundations. You tap into a pathway that nourishes your life on multiple levels, marking a turning point that helps you reach an uptick of potential. You can open the floodgates and embrace gaining traction on improving your circumstances as you enter a cycle of increased possibility. It offers a more connected environment that promotes social inclusion.

## 15 Wednesday

Mercury settles into Taurus; your thinking is down to earth, balanced, and grounded. It is a good time for establishing your talents and achieving growth, security, and progression. Leaning into the added demands on your time helps you lead with your strengths. It is a fluid and changing environment that brings challenges and potential. Working with your abilities enables you to shine as those above take notice of your adequate and efficient track record.

## 16 Thursday

Developing a strategy and designing unique goals for your career path become the building blocks that offer growth and progress. Opportunities ahead positively show that things are ready for development and progression. Nurturing your abilities and developing your skills brings your gifts to a broader audience. You enter a busy time in your working life. It increases your knowledge base and enables you to advance to greener pastures.

**17 Friday**

You soon reveal a touch of magic that arrives to bless your life with a more social environment. Opportunities to mingle lift the lid on a curious time of expanding your circle of friends. It helps you break fresh ground by increasing your circle of friends as communication arrives to link you up with social activities. Harnessing the possibilities available in your life lets you explore options that offer a golden phase of rising potential.

**18 Saturday**

Venus teams up with Uranus to add a dash of spontaneity to your social/personal life. Another conjunct occurs between the Sun and Jupiter, adding lightness and momentum to your life. You enter a time of rising prospects in your social life. Pushing back the barriers improves your life's foundations and offers new opportunities that connect you with people who nourish your spirit and bring a positive outcome.

**19 Sunday**

Building grounded foundations and dabbling in your hobbies offers a therapeutic influence that nurtures your spirit. Creating space to make your home life a sanctuary promotes well-being and stability. It translates to a chapter that renews and rebuilds the foundations of your life. It does link you to a happy and rewarding time that enriches life with grounded foundations that draw renewal. Enjoying a leisurely pace places you in the correct alignment to promote harmony.

## 20 Monday

Being methodical and diligent with effective use of your time will enable you to gain traction on a stellar week of high performance. As you improve your circumstances, you draw greater security, promoting grounded foundations. Opportunity comes knocking, shifting your focus forward towards advancing your talents. You discover curious options ripe with potential, and designing the path ahead helps you make tracks toward growing your life.

## 21 Tuesday

Newfound motivation fuels inspiration as you launch toward developing an endeavor that promotes rising innovation and creativity. You enter a phase of growing your life and expanding your reach into a new area. It takes you on a journey that deepens your knowledge and cultivates advancement in your life. Taking your abilities to the next level sees you come out the other side with new skills and a focus on growing life.

## 22 Wednesday

The Sun trine Pluto aspect increases your desire to gain power and drive your ambitious streak to greater heights. You head towards rising prospects that open up opportunities to grow your career. It offers a gateway towards progression as you get busy working with your abilities and unlock the next step forward for your career path. You lay the groundwork for a suitable time for developing your working life. A bright and breezy environment brings new energy ahead.

## 23 Thursday

Today's Venus conjunct Jupiter aspect is a positive sign for your social life. Venus harmonizes bonds and draws a dreamy vibe when she forms a sextile with Neptune. The Venus ingress into Gemini draws balanced energy, which nurtures your romantic and social life. As Gemini adds lightness and harmony to conversations, Venus is the perfect companion which links up to growth around your tribe. Conversations are light, breezy, and fun, boosting your life.

### 24 Friday

A more social environment ignites inspiration and leads to lively discussions. An invitation to catch up with friends draws excitement. The conversations ahead pull a valuable sense of connection and open a joyful journey. You are undergoing a time of transition that kicks open a fresh chapter in your life. It brings the rising aspect to your social life that has you dreaming about the possibilities. It opens life to an exciting flavor as you get busy with goals that promote happy foundations.

### 25 Saturday

Venus trine Pluto brings an increasing drive that adds intensity as it has you focusing on developing future goals sooner rather than later. Jupiter's ingress Gemini is a favorable planetary aspect that promotes harmony. It brings fresh air into your surroundings and a light and breezy vibe that feels good for your soul. The future looks rosy as you soon open a social time that offers a curious path forward for your life. It hits a sweet note that nurtures a unique journey.

### 26 Sunday

A social aspect ahead sparks a path that governs well-being and harmony. Improving life releases stress and brings the gift of companionship to your door. Sharing with companions profoundly stabilizes and restores balance to the foundations of your home life. Good fortune beckons as you discover a lively environment that promotes growth in your circle of friends. It opens a journey that draws connection and companionship.

### 27 Monday

You are on track to improving your circumstances. Designing a life that captures the essence of imagination takes you to a radiant time where you use your gifts of self-expression and creativity to increase the prospects in your life. There is much improvement at the crux of the upcoming developments as life becomes attractive with expansion and increases occurring in your social life. It brings engaging discussions and lively moments shared with friends.

### 28 Tuesday

With Mercury in sextile with Saturn, communication skills are rising. Enhanced clarity help with concepts, thought processes, and ideas. This cosmic enhancement enables you to step beyond traditional learning and take your studies/working life to the next level. It lets you expand your horizons into areas that deepen your knowledge and grow your abilities. New possibilities raise confidence and bring a newfound energy to develop projects of meaning.

### 29 Wednesday

Clues ahead help you reveal a rising possibility that brings an upgrade into your life. Being open to developing new leads generates potential worth your time. It opens a busy and productive journey that promotes new projects. It opens a path that creates room to build your skills. Incoming changes enable you to make notable tracks to improve your life's foundations. It helps you clear away the blocks and expand your horizons by proactively growing your life outwardly.

### 30 Thursday

As something special makes a grand entrance into your life, it awakens creativity and brings vitality, offering a welcome boost. Notable changes highlight an enriching path that provides a unique approach. It helps you get busy focusing on your priorities. Effectively channeling your energy brings rising prospects to the surface. It activates a driven chapter that brings the ideal conditions to work with your skills and create a progressive shift toward growth.

# JUNE

| Sun | Mon | Tue | Wed | Thu | Fri | Sat |
|-----|-----|-----|-----|-----|-----|-----|
|     |     |     |     |     |     | 1   |
| 2   | 3   | 4   | 5   | 6   | 7   | 8   |
| 9   | 10  | 11  | 12  | 13  | 14  | 15  |
| 16  | 17  | 18  | 19  | 20  | 21  | 22  |
| 23  | 24  | 25  | 26  | 27  | 28  | 29  |
| 30  |     |     |     |     |     |     |

# NEW MOON

# STRAWBERRY MOON

**31 Friday**

Mercury and Uranus form a positive aspect that heightens mental abilities. Increasing mental stimulation promotes fresh ideas in your life today. Technology, messages, and communication all spark inspiration and foster possibilities for future development. Collaboration, brainstorming and working with others to achieve your chosen destination become a strong emphasis. You touch down in a supportive environment that provides room to grow your talents.

**1 Saturday**

Jupiter trine Pluto transit improves confidence and brings a powerful influence that helps you exert your power to gain control over developing your vision for future growth. You will feel more in control over the passage ahead and be able to use your mastery to obtain positive results in your life. Being confident, enthusiastic, and capable draws rising potential. A new path looms overhead and enables you to advance towards a brighter chapter in your working life.

**2 Sunday**

You receive some uplifting news that brings positive changes to your social life. Opportunities for connection and conversation with like-minded individuals are boosting your well-being and happiness. Spending time with family strengthens your bonds and contributes to a happier outlook. Embrace this new, more connected phase for maximum pleasure and fulfillment. Take advantage of this time and cultivate these relationships for continued growth and happiness.

JUNE
---

**3 Monday**

The Mercury sextile Neptune blends rational thinking with a dreamy aspect. It brings rising creativity and analytical thinking, promoting epiphanies that count. This cosmic alignment helps your dreams become a reality as structured backing behind your vision offers tangible results. Mercury ingress Gemini brings news and information, which adds a refreshing aspect. Communication is light and lively, adding fresh air to your surroundings.

**4 Tuesday**

Mercury trine Pluto attracts a questioning aspect that encourages you to dig deeper. Delving into what motivates you on a deeper level proves illuminating today. Sun conjunct Venus transit brings peaceful energy, promoting harmony and focusing on your love relationships and personal bonds. It draws a warm and enchanting journey for your romantic life. The future looks rosy as you land in a fascinating landscape that draws romance and magic into your life.

**5 Wednesday**

You can embrace new opportunities and seek experiences that challenge and stretch you. Collaborate with others and build meaningful relationships that bring positivity and support. Don't be afraid to take calculated risks and explore new avenues, as this is a time for growth and development. Stay organized and prioritize your time, balancing your personal and professional life in a way that brings you happiness and fulfillment.

**6 Thursday**

The New Moon offers a chance to think about the coming month and plan goals that progress life forward. Setting intentions and thinking about your future aspirations help connect with the energy of manifestation to achieve a pleasing result. It ignites new possibilities as life heads to an exciting upswing allowing you to reap the rewards of expansion. Designing dreams and crafting your vision for future growth brings a rewarding outcome to your door.

84

**7 Friday**

A positive change offers growth in various aspects of your life. The arrival of exciting options opens up new opportunities and leads you toward a more stable and fulfilling future. Focus on creating plans and taking action toward your interests and goals. Building and expanding your social network brings happiness, confidence, and community. Embrace the positive changes and allow yourself to enjoy the process of growth and discovery.

**8 Saturday**

A social aspect hits a sweet note: Developing relationships with others enrich life and brings a positive flow of energy into your world. It opens the door to new opportunities and provides a platform for growth. You will feel encouraged to be more expressive and generous, which can foster deeper connections and bring happiness to your life. The positive influences ahead allow you to explore new avenues and bring stability to your life.

**9 Sunday**

Mars ingress Taurus focuses on long-term projects as you work slowly and methodically to achieve your goals. This transit emphasizes the value of hard work and patience as you build towards a better future. Take a long-term perspective, and focus on projects that will bring lasting benefits. Prioritize stability and security, both in your personal and professional life. Stay disciplined and consistent, and put in the time and effort required to achieve your goals.

JUNE

**10 Monday**

New information cracks the code to a brighter chapter. This unique opportunity can help you gain more exposure and increase your self-confidence. Embracing change and stepping out of your comfort zone can lead to personal growth and success. The upcoming chapter can bring excitement and a chance to shine as you showcase your abilities. Focus on making the most of this opportunity and let it lead you toward a brighter future.

**11 Tuesday**

Mars square Pluto transit brings workplace power struggles and competition. It is a problematic planetary transit that can feel jarring. However, you won't have to worry about competition as your work will shine above any detractors. It brings a spectacular time that has you eager to gain traction in developing your dreams. You nail progress that offers growth and progress. Setting your sights on your chosen destination rings in a successful outcome ahead.

**12 Wednesday**

A new chapter of growth and expansion is beginning, providing opportunities to showcase your skills and explore your creative abilities. This period of change will bring new connections and chances for progress, allowing you to build a solid foundation for your future. Embrace this moment, stay focused on your goals, and you will surely succeed. With opportunities on the horizon, it's time to take bold steps toward realizing your dreams and building a brighter future.

**13 Thursday**

Exciting changes ahead bring growth, advancement, and new opportunities to your life. You can capitalize on your skills and interests, opening the door to a more fulfilling and prosperous future. The journey towards growth and improvement offers a positive and energetic outlook, allowing you to connect with others and build a supportive network of friends and allies. Embrace this dynamic and transformative time to create a brighter, more meaningful chapter in your life.

**14 Friday**

In conjunction with Mercury, the Sun is a favorable aspect that attracts communication. News arrives that brings a social invitation your way. You enter a highly social element that brings a focus on developing friendships. It triggers a path of expansion that spotlights responsive and thoughtful communication, building grounded foundations around your life. Under this more social environment, you discover room to embrace a connected vibe.

**15 Saturday**

Seek new opportunities and be open to meeting new people who share your passions. The social aspect of this journey will add to the overall experience and bring balance to your life. Don't be afraid to take risks; embrace change and be curious. Remember, growth comes from stepping outside your comfort zone and trying new things. So enjoy the ride, stay focused on your goals, and have fun along the way.

**16 Sunday**

Take time to research and gain knowledge, participate in events and activities that interest you, and seek new experiences. Surround yourself with like-minded individuals who share your passions and support your growth. Remember to balance your pursuit of knowledge and exploration with rest and self-care. Your mental and emotional well-being are as important as your growth. Embrace new adventures, trust the journey, and enjoy the process of expanding your horizons.

### 17 Monday

Today, the Mercury square Neptune aspect can distort or make mountains of molehills. It adds a dash of illusion into your business dealings that can have your head spinning with tall tales and trying to sort the truth from exaggeration. This area is one of those days that tempt you to expand the barriers and think outside the box to develop workable solutions. Venus slips into Cancer to encourage a focus on emotional well-being and personal bonds.

### 18 Tuesday

A stimulating environment opens doors for you to develop new skills and experiences, leading to personal growth. Embrace opportunities, take calculated risks, stay open-minded, and focus on continuous improvement. Surround yourself with positive and supportive people who inspire and challenge you. The journey toward success and fulfillment is ongoing, so keep pushing yourself to reach new heights and make the most of each day.

### 19 Wednesday

New information signals a time for building stronger relationships and expanding your social circle. You can take advantage of the invitations and engage with others in meaningful and enjoyable experiences. Focus on bringing positivity and energy to each interaction, and be open to forming new connections. Remember to balance your social life with self-care and alone time. Your social links significantly affect your overall well-being, so invest in them wisely.

### 20 Thursday

Today, the Neptune square Sun aspect can water down your ambitions, leaving you feeling foggy and indecisive. The Neptune square Sun aspect can create confusion and uncertainty, making it challenging to stay focused on your goals. You may feel your plans are unclear or your motivation is lacking. If your vision feels clouded, going back over your dreams can help ensure they align with your vision for future growth.

### 21 Friday

A sextile between Mercury and Mars sharpens cognitive abilities today. Mental clarity is on the rise, giving you valuable insight into the path ahead. You enter a phase of growing your life and expanding your reach into a new area. It takes you on a journey that deepens your knowledge and cultivates advancement in your life. Taking your abilities to the next level sees you develop new skills and a focus on growing in life. Celebrating successes along the way keeps inspiration firing.

### 22 Saturday

The Full Moon brings awareness into your spirit of the areas that seek resolution or adjustment. A time of contemplation draws clarity into the path ahead. It helps you sweep away the outworn areas that hold no future benefits. Taking time to think about things on a deeper level puts you in touch with deep emotions that open healing in your life. It underscores an atmosphere of personal growth that puts you on a path toward your higher calling.

### 23 Sunday

You can embrace the excitement and take advantage of new opportunities that come your way. Being proactive in setting and achieving your goals; helps you dream big. Focusing on personal and professional development lets, you stay optimistic about the future. It is an exciting time, so enjoy the journey and make the most of each day. Success and fulfillment are a journey, not just a destination, so enjoy each step. Staying positive helps you not lose sight of your dreams.

**24 Monday**

New information sets you on a path of discovery and learning, leading to personal growth and an enhanced sense of well-being. You find new ways to express yourself and bring your unique talents to the forefront. Your environment improves and supports your growth, providing the necessary space and resources to achieve your goals. You find joy in nurturing relationships and fostering a sense of community, bringing fulfillment and happiness to your life.

**25 Tuesday**

Today opens new doors to exciting possibilities, growth, and fulfillment. You are ready to take a leap of faith into a brighter future, and the rewards of your hard work are starting to show. You find a new sense of purpose and direction as you bring your skills to the forefront and make your mark on the world. The more you focus on improving your life, the more you tap into resources that support your dreams and bring joy and happiness.

**26 Wednesday**

News arrives that opens the gate to an uptick of potential in your life. You get a glimpse of a prestigious area that comes calling to advance life forward. This new opportunity is a stepping stone to reaching new heights and realizing your full potential. Embracing change and putting in the effort to pursue your passions can bring great rewards and satisfaction in the long run. Stay focused and driven toward your goals, and you'll see growth and success in your life.

**27 Thursday**

As you develop new skills, you create a solid foundation for growth and prosperity. It brings a sense of purpose and direction to your life, and you are eager to explore new horizons that advance your life. Your progress motivates you to continue growing and expanding your abilities, which sets the stage for a brighter future. As you cultivate change and explore new possibilities, you'll move toward a prosperous path filled with growth, learning, and increased security.

**28 Friday**

Stay positive and be proactive, taking steps towards your vision every day. Be open to new experiences, and don't be afraid to try new things. Stay disciplined and stay true to your values, and you'll be able to navigate this time of change with confidence and determination. Embrace the journey and trust that you are on the right path. Remember to continue to grow and develop skills. With hard work and persistence, you'll be able to create a fulfilling and prosperous future.

**29 Saturday**

Venus's sextile with Mars draws social engagement into your life. It opens the floodgates to an enriching time that brings invitations to circulate with friends and kindred spirits. A buzz of activity ahead attracts romance and thoughtful discussions. Saturn turns retrograde; this aspect focuses on the areas that hold the most significant meaning in your life. As you chart a course toward developing new leads, a sense of possibility drives your vision.

**30 Sunday**

This time highlights growth and expansion in personal and social life. The focus is on networking with friends and building new relationships. Investing time and energy in personal growth and development can create fulfillment and purpose. The emphasis on improving your home life can bring stability and security. Expanding your social circle brings new opportunities for companionship and support. You soon embrace a happier and more fulfilling life.

# July

| Sun | Mon | Tue | Wed | Thu | Fri | Sat |
|-----|-----|-----|-----|-----|-----|-----|
|     | 1   | 2   | 3   | 4   | 5   | 6   |
| 7   | 8   | 9   | 10  | 11  | 12  | 13  |
| 14  | 15  | 16  | 17  | 18  | 19  | 20  |
| 21  | 22  | 23  | 24  | 25  | 26  | 27  |
| 28  | 29  | 30  | 31  |     |     |     |

# NEW MOON

# BUCK MOON

# JULY

### 1 Monday

A change on the horizon brings new opportunities and possibilities for growth. This week is a time to take control of your life and reshuffle the deck of potential, positioning yourself for success and prosperity. Let your creativity flourish and inspire your spirit as you develop your goals. Focusing on your plans and purpose brings a sense of direction and motivation, allowing you to move confidently. Remember to stay optimistic and trust that the universe works in your favor.

### 2 Tuesday

Turning retrograde today, Neptune strips away illusion and any dubious realities which have clouded your vision. At the same time, the Mercury trine Neptune transit stimulates creativity and imagination and fine-tunes your instincts. Mercury ingress Leo adds an expressive vibe that enhances your storytelling and persuasive abilities. Use this transit to tap into your creative potential and communicate your ideas effectively, and you can make positive changes.

### 3 Wednesday

Your relationships and social bonds benefit from a steady stream of balanced energy as the Venus trine Saturn contributes loving harmony to your life. Mercury opposed Pluto increases cognitive abilities. It is the perfect transit for researching, developing business ideas, and applying an innovative approach to improving your circumstances. Focus on your priorities and ensure that your efforts lean toward your most important goals.

### 4 Thursday

Exciting times as new opportunities bring growth and fulfillment to your social life. Focusing on building relationships attracts supportive and rewarding outcomes, leading to new adventures and strengthening existing friendships. Get ready for a busy and dynamic time filled with positive developments. It opens opportunities to grow and build meaningful connections. Pursuing growth and joy brings positive changes that enhance your well-being and confidence.

**5 Friday**

Mars sextile sat Saturn adds endurance today, helping you accomplish mundane tasks and keep productive. A New Moon provides the ideal opportunity to map a plan for future growth. This New Moon is a call to honor your creativity as tapping into your wildest instincts rejuvenates and revolutionizes your life by carving out a journey that speaks to your soul. Nurturing your skills and dabbling in unique areas brings creativity, passion, and inspiration.

**6 Saturday**

You open a path toward growth and expansion. Sharing experiences and thoughts with others can bring new perspectives and social engagement. This time of change can positively impact your social life and emotional well-being. Discovering new interests or activities that bring joy and fulfillment can fuel your emotional tank. The increased social and personal growth can get a brighter outlook and attract new opportunities for growth and happiness.

**7 Sunday**

A significant change and opportunity for growth emerge. Discovering a new endeavor or project worth pursuing brings purpose and fulfillment. The theme of improving your life opens doors to new possibilities and growth. This new chapter gives a sense of enrichment and the opportunity to lay a strong foundation for a bright future. Embrace this time of transition as an opportunity to chart a new course toward growth, happiness, and personal development.

### 8 Monday

Open-mindedness, curiosity, and a quest for adventure are prominent aspects as a Mercury sextile Jupiter alignment fosters creativity and self-expression. It does help you achieve remarkable growth as your talents become stronger and influence the trajectory of your vision for future growth. You put your foot forward in a progressive environment by leveraging challenges and utilizing your skills. New assignments bring opportunities for collaboration.

### 9 Tuesday

Notable changes ahead transform life into a busy time. It brings an approach that offers positivity as you mark a turning point and expand life outwardly. Exploring leads jumpstarts growth and helps you push back the barriers to achieve a successful outcome. You take your talents into uncharted territory and upscale your skills, bringing new options to light. You hone in on rising potential that takes your gifts to a new level.

### 10 Wednesday

Focusing on the foundations of your life leads to growth and increased security. A willingness to embrace change and explore new opportunities helps you reach new heights and advance your talents into areas that bring fulfilling results. Evaluating the direction ahead and making bold choices help you realize your potential and achieve your goals. Make the most of this time by working on the foundations and pursuing options that improve security and promote growth.

### 11 Thursday

Venus trine Neptune transit attracts creativity, well-being, and fulfillment. Venus makes a bold statement as she gets comfy in Leo. It is a warm, expressive, generous time. It is a time to embrace your creativity and let positive energy flow. You may feel a heightened passion and romanticism, making it a great time to enjoy the finer things and connect with others on a deeper level. Take advantage of this transit to experience greater joy, beauty, and fulfillment.

### 12 Friday

Jealousy may surface as relationships face extra pressure today due to opposition between Pluto and Venus. This transit can reveal insecurities and power struggles within relationships. It may be a time to confront these issues and work towards resolving any conflicts. To strive for a balance of power and equality in your relationships is essential. Use this time to reflect on your relationships' underlying motivations and dynamics and make efforts towards understanding and growth.

### 13 Saturday

With new prospects and positive energy, your life takes on a new direction as you move forward with growing opportunities. Your focus on relationships opens doors to learning, growth, and excitement. The possibilities are endless as you make great strides toward creating a happier, more fulfilling life. New experiences and connections allow you to embrace joy and abundance, leading you to a brighter future filled with endless potential.

### 14 Sunday

You connect with like-minded individuals and develop a supportive network of friends who help you expand your horizons and chase your passions. It leads to a fulfilling chapter of growth, learning, and personal development, as you embark on an exciting journey toward your goals and aspirations. An uplift in your social life presents opportunities for personal growth and positive change. It creates a supportive environment for new experiences and the exchange of ideas.

**15 Monday**

Mars conjunct Uranus aspect lets you become more aware of motivations and values and discover the real reasons behind wants and desires. This aspect can bring change and independence in one's thinking and behavior. It can lead to breaking free from old patterns and embracing new, unconventional ideas and ways of living. It brings excitement and unpredictability, but this aspect also offers growth and innovation.

**16 Tuesday**

A new start provides an ideal platform to explore new opportunities that bring growth, happiness, and prosperity into your life. It fosters a positive outlook and the willingness to take risks, which opens new doors and brings in new perspectives. With the proper support and positive energy, you can achieve great things and turn your dreams into reality. It marks a time of personal growth, happiness, and success.

**17 Wednesday**

Taking advantage of new opportunities draws an exciting time of growth and expansion in your career. It opens doors to increased stability and helps you build the foundations for a secure future. Exploring new horizons in your work life nurtures an atmosphere of abundance that attracts positive outcomes and enhances your financial stability. Embracing change and pursuing your passions helps create a fulfilling and prosperous career path.

**18 Thursday**

You can trust that your hard work will lead to a bright future, attracting new opportunities, growth, and success in your professional life. You can reach your full potential and create your desired future with focus and determination. By embracing change and adapting to new circumstances, you build a strong foundation for success. With increased productivity, you attract positive outcomes and move forward with confidence.

**19 Friday**

News arrives, which highlights an opportunity for growth and development. Focusing on your strengths and abilities can help you maximize this potential and create new opportunities for success. This unique opportunity may bring a bright and exciting chapter filled with new experiences and growth. The revelation may add to your motivation and inspire you to manifest your goals and aspirations. Embrace this chance to make positive changes and advance your ambitions.

**20 Saturday**

Mars settles into Gemini, which encourages a more diverse outlook. It helps you discover the hidden pathways and journey toward growth over the coming two months. Mars in Gemini brings energy and determination to intellectual and communication activities. This transit encourages a curious and open-minded approach, leading to new perspectives and opportunities. With this influence, you can try new things, meet new people, and explore different ideas.

**21 Sunday**

The Full Moon is a chance for therapeutic healing in your life. If you face a crossroads in your life, going deeper into your goals and aspirations helps provide insight into the path ahead. You are entering a time that rules endings and transitions; it opens a new chapter that acts as a catalyst for change. Thinking about your life on a deeper level is therapeutic as it facilitates a healing influence. An area you invest time and energy into developing promotes happiness.

**22 Monday**

A Venus and Jupiter sextile attracts warm and abundant energy into your social life. A dash of luck and good fortune combined with enriching conversations improve social bonds in your life. Original thinking, creative brainstorming, and insightful epiphanies are the order of the day as Mercury squares off against Uranus today. Something new and inspiring flows into your life. The Sun trine Neptune alignment raises the vibration and improves circumstances in your life.

**23 Tuesday**

The Sun's opposition with Pluto creates a doorway through which pockets of the inner self, spirit, and primal energy can reach the surface of your awareness. This aspect can highlight the need for personal transformation and the release of outdated behaviors and beliefs. However, with determination and self-awareness, this aspect can bring growth and empowerment. It can be a time of powerful personal transformation and liberation of one's inner self and genuine spirit.

**24 Wednesday**

A new chapter in your life brings motivation and excitement as you strive to reach new heights. You focus on maximizing your strengths and increasing your sense of purpose and direction. Embracing growth and learning opportunities provides a rewarding experience and sets you on the path to success. The future looks bright as you pursue your passions and progress toward your goals. You can achieve your dreams by focusing on growth, learning, and accomplishment.

**25 Thursday**

Mercury links up with Gemini, emphasizing connecting with your tribe. Mercury in Gemini is known to enhance communication and mental agility. This transit may bring a focus on connecting with others and gathering information. This transit can also get a desire to learn and exchange ideas with others, making it a good time for networking and meeting new people. Overall, this transit can be a time of productive and stimulating communication and personal growth.

**26 Friday**

The Sun's sextile Mars transit brings vital energy and renewed zest for life. This transit can be a great time to tackle new projects and pursue your goals with renewed determination. You'll likely feel more confident, assertive, and eager to take on new challenges. Embrace this transit to reignite your drive and get moving toward the things that bring you joy and fulfillment. With this burst of energy and motivation, you'll be well-equipped to tackle anything that comes your way.

**27 Saturday**

The path ahead becomes more apparent as you build meaningful relationships with people who understand and support your goals. The journey forward brings new opportunities for growth, learning, and self-expression. You find fulfillment as you connect with like-minded individuals who inspire and motivate you to reach new heights. The road ahead looks bright and promising, filled with endless potential for growth, adventure, and success.

**28 Sunday**

Your social network grows, providing diverse perspectives that broaden your horizons. This upward trend in your social life marks a new chapter of growth and adventure. It brings a time of exploring new connections, friendships, and experiences that broaden your horizons and uplift your mood. Opportunities to express yourself and engage in lively conversations fuel your passion and creativity.

# AUGUST

| Sun | Mon | Tue | Wed | Thu | Fri | Sat |
|-----|-----|-----|-----|-----|-----|-----|
|     |     |     |     | 1   | 2   | 3   |
| 4   | 5   | 6   | 7   | 8   | 9   | 10  |
| 11  | 12  | 13  | 14  | 15  | 16  | 17  |
| 18  | 19  | 20  | 21  | 22  | 23  | 24  |
| 25  | 26  | 27  | 28  | 29  | 30  | 31  |

# NEW MOON

# STURGEON MOON

**29 Monday**

You're on a path to greater productivity and success in your career. Nurturing your skills and abilities brings positive developments and opportunities to grow your financial stability. Your hard work pays off, leading to prosperity and growth in your professional life. Your energy and determination lead the way toward a bright future filled with opportunities. Embrace this time of change and make the most of it, as it lays the foundation for a successful future.

**30 Tuesday**

As you focus on advancing your skills, new opportunities arise that bring growth and prosperity. Your hard work and determination pay off as you secure new projects and contracts, allowing you to further establish your reputation and expertise. The future looks bright as you progress and strive toward your vision of success. Stay the course and keep pushing forward, as the rewards of your efforts are just around the corner.

**31 Wednesday**

A new chapter opens in your working life unfolds, filled with growth opportunities and increased productivity. You tap into your potential and focus on developing your skills, which leads to recognition and success. With a positive outlook and an eagerness to learn, you are well-positioned to climb the ladder of success and achieve your goals. It is a time of growth and accomplishment as you create a strong foundation for a bright and prosperous future.

**1 Thursday**

As you focus on developing your skills and exploring new opportunities, your working life becomes more fulfilling and prosperous. The hard work and dedication pay off as you achieve new levels of success and recognition in your field. It is a time of growth and progress where you can truly shine and make a difference in your career. So keep pushing forward and embracing new challenges, as this period of growth and achievement holds endless possibilities for you.

**2 Friday**

An increased need for freedom and liberation can destabilize bonds as Venus faces Uranus in a square alignment. Remember to shake off heavy vibrations during this planetary transit and release stress as you kick drama to the curb. It is a highly creative time that lets you spark ideas and plans for future development. An opportunity for collaboration helps settle frazzled nerves; it brings a group environment into focus that promotes greater harmony in your circle.

**3 Saturday**

As you tap into new opportunities, a creative spark ignites, pushing you toward fulfilling experiences and achievements. Your social network expands, and new connections bring new insights and perspectives, enabling growth and progression. The support of your friends amplifies your confidence, allowing you to take on new challenges and thrive in your endeavors. This positive energy cultivates an environment of growth, which fuels your future success.

**4 Sunday**

The New Moon offers a chance to boost your intentions, which can assist you with working with the universe's energy to manifest your goals. This New Moon focuses on honoring your creativity, so take this as a chance to tap into your wildest instincts and bring a new level of excitement and energy to your life. By following your passions and listening to your soul, you can revolutionize your life and carve out a journey that is uniquely yours.

### 5 Monday

Venus ingress Virgo emphasizes practical matters as you build more excellent stability in your home life. Friendly times shared with friends and family result in unexpected possibilities that improve your life prospects. It allows you to expand your circle. Seeing improvement in your social life brings newfound confidence. Life dazzles in increasing joy, happiness, and connection with others. It opens an upward trend that promotes the chasing of dreams.

### 6 Tuesday

You find opportunities to refine your skills and improve your talents, which opens doors to a more productive work environment and attracts recognition from those around you. Your hard work and dedication pay off as you build a strong foundation for continued growth and advancement in your career. Your upward trajectory brings a bright future filled with endless possibilities for success and fulfillment.

### 7 Wednesday

In sextile with Jupiter, the Sun attracts a restless vibe that has you yearning to expand your life outwardly. Exciting possibilities set the stage for a new journey that promotes creativity. A lush green landscape of potential helps you weave and design a path toward unique goals. You open a connected social environment that facilitates expansion. Expanding the borders of life shines a spotlight on increasing happiness. It earmarks an exciting time that brings a busy aspect.

### 8 Thursday

Mercury conjunct Venus brings the right time to share loving thoughts and receive positive feedback from someone who holds meaning in your life. You let your hair down and communicate openly. It brings a sense of support and connection that draws enrichment. It offers a social environment, and sharing with companions brings discussions that initiate unique possibilities. It marks an important time for being involved with others, and this openness gets your life on track as you grow.

**9 Friday**

Lively discussions and brainstorming sessions spark innovative ideas and result in collaborative projects that bring your ideas to life. As you grow your tribe, you'll gain a support system that will encourage you to reach new heights. This time of heightened sociability can also bring a sense of fulfillment and happiness as you create meaningful connections with others. So continue to put yourself out there, engage in lively conversations, and never stop learning and growing.

**10 Saturday**

Your proactive attitude attracts new opportunities and opens up a path of growth. New prospects bring a time of learning and improvement as you take your life to the next level. With a fresh outlook, you move forward, engaging with others and building meaningful connections. Your social life flourishes and you create a supportive network that nurtures your growth. It marks a turning point as you embrace change and chase dreams with excitement and confidence.

**11 Sunday**

New information sets the stage for a productive time as you expand your social circle and connect with like-minded people. The growth of your social life brings new energy and opportunities to explore your interests and talents. A supportive environment fosters a positive outlook, allowing you to pursue your passions and reach your goals. The journey ahead promises to be exciting, inspiring, and full of growth, bringing you closer to realizing your full potential.

### 12 Monday

Opportunity comes knocking and opens your life to new flavors and possibilities. You reveal areas that tempt you to use your talents and work with your skills to advance life. It sees creativity blooming, and working with your abilities places you in the proper alignment to reach a golden avenue of possibility. Being open to change is the giver of gifts and good fortune; it links you with others who offer a supportive and group environment.

### 13 Tuesday

A golden aspect weaves through your life, bringing good news. Something unique on offer takes your talents to the next level. Building a course towards your dreams amplifies potential and offers a remarkable shift forward. You invest time and energy into developing a path that holds water and soon blossoms into a sound journey ahead. Advancement is in the pipeline; a new initiative brings a busy and progressive time.

### 14 Wednesday

Today's Mars conjunct Jupiter transit is ideal for developing goals that require focused energy, initiative, and confidence. This transit can bring a sense of expansion and growth and be a great time to plan for the future. With this energy behind you, you can make significant progress towards your goals, so embrace this transit to make the most of the opportunities that come your way. It is ideal for developing plans that require focused energy, initiative, and a sense of purpose.

### 15 Thursday

Mercury gets comfy in Leo and brings rising confidence that imbues you with persuasive abilities and an expressive spark that improves communication skills. This transit can help you tap into your inner voice and communicate your ideas, allowing you to articulate your thoughts and opinions easily. Your persuasive skills heighten, giving you the power to influence others and make your case effectively. It is excellent for projects that require communication skills.

**16 Friday**

Today's aspect can feel challenging as your mind is on Saturn's to-do list. You may find it difficult to relax and unwind when your thoughts turn to the irons you have burning in the fire. Stay focused on your goals, and remember to care for yourself mentally and physically. Trust your instincts and believe in yourself. Take calculated risks and always learn from your experiences. Keep growing and pushing your limits; you'll be on your way to a fulfilling and prosperous future.

**17 Saturday**

Don't be afraid to step outside your comfort zone and try new things. Network and build connections with others. Seek out new experiences and learn from the diverse perspectives of those around you. Remember to have fun and enjoy the journey. Stay focused on your goals, but don't forget to celebrate your achievements and successes. With positivity, hard work, and determination, you will continue to create a fulfilling life full of adventure and joyful connections.

**18 Sunday**

Original thinking, creative brainstorming, and insightful epiphanies are the order of the day as Mercury squares off against Uranus today. Something new and inspiring flows into your life. However, this transit can also lead to scattered energy and impulsive decisions, so it's essential to approach this time with diligence and mindfulness. So let your mind wander and embrace this transit's new and exciting possibilities.

**19 Monday**

Independent thinking and innovative ideas are attributable to the Sun and Mercury conjunct. Today's Venus square Jupiter planetary alignment offers good things for your social life. It is the perfect time to engage with friends; lively discussions nurture creativity. Lastly, the Full Moon brings the chance to clean the slate and heal sensitive areas. Creating space to engage with a healing ritual, such as playing soft music or lighting a candle, helps nurture therapeutic influence.

**20 Tuesday**

You get involved in developing a dream project. Research ahead helps design plans that light up areas of creativity, potential, and growth. News arrives that enables you to take tangible steps toward outlining strategies and building your dreams. Setting intentions fuels your spirit and restocks the tank of inspiration. Nourishing the seeds of creativity brings a blossoming time of working with your abilities to achieve a robust result.

**21 Wednesday**

News arrives that gives you a brighter picture of the path ahead. It draws new options that bring a busy and productive time for developing goals and working with your talents. You enter a goal-orientated phase of designing strategic plans and expanding life. Unique prospects ahead offer golden returns on your time. As momentum gathers, you discover an upgrade that brings excitement and joy. It brings forward-facing speed that provides room to grow your life.

**22 Thursday**

A new phase of growth and development in your working life will bring a sense of fulfillment and satisfaction. The skills and experience you gain will be valuable assets that you can use to achieve future goals and aspirations. The opportunities that come your way will help you advance and reach new heights of success. You can expect positive outcomes and growth as you continue to put effort into your work and strive towards your aspirations.

**23 Friday**

A Venus square Mars aspect can cause challenges as a difference of opinion fosters tension and conflict. Being mindful of staying flexible, understanding, and adaptive will help harmonize bonds and limit the disruption caused by Venus facing Mars at a harsh angle. Being willing to compromise will improve the foundations and limit the disruption in your life. It brings a time of letting go of areas that restrict progress.

**24 Saturday**

A new phase opens a time of growth, connection, and meaningful conversations with those who share similar passions and interests. You attract positive energy and opportunities, leading to a more fulfilling social life and a more profound sense of community. Your creative spirit shines, inspiring you to pursue your dreams and pursue new adventures. It is a time to trust the journey and embrace the growth that comes with expanding your horizons and connecting with others.

**25 Sunday**

A time of growth and progress awaits as you tap into your creativity and focus on what brings joy to your life. Opportunities for new connections and adventures arise, helping you expand your social network and create meaningful relationships. You feel inspired and empowered, ready to pursue your goals and dreams confidently. Your energy attracts positive outcomes and sets you on a path of growth and fulfillment.

### 26 Monday

You see growth and improvement as you focus on your skills and abilities. New doors open, offering opportunities to advance your career and reach new heights. Your hard work and dedication pay off as you experience success and recognition in your field. With a focus on your goals, you reap the benefits of your hard work and determination. Your life is in a cycle of progression and improvement, and opportunities for growth and success are abundant.

### 27 Tuesday

By leveraging your strengths and putting in the hard work, you see a rise in success, recognition, and prosperity. The path ahead is exciting and filled with opportunities for growth and learning, offering you a chance to make your mark in the world. With determination, focus, and drive, you are poised to reach new heights and achieve your greatest aspirations. The journey holds the potential for substantial rewards and recognition for your hard work and dedication.

### 28 Wednesday

Mercury turns direct, bringing a lighter energy flow into your social life. This planetary transit can help to clarify misunderstandings and resolve any miscommunications that may have arisen during the retrograde phase. As a result, your relationships may become stronger and more positive as you can express yourself more effectively and connect with others on a deeper level. Additionally, the improved flow of energy can lead to new opportunities for collaboration.

### 29 Thursday

Venus settles into Libra, raising communication in your life. Personal bonds sweeten, you share ideas, and the opportunity for collaboration heightens. Today's Venus trine with Pluto adds intensity to your love life. This aspect turns up the heat in your personal life. Sexual attraction and passion rise as you get busy developing your personal life. Singles will likely find new romance soon, while couples can embrace a more connected and sizzling love life.

# SEPTEMBER

| Sun | Mon | Tue | Wed | Thu | Fri | Sat |
|-----|-----|-----|-----|-----|-----|-----|
| 1 | 2 | 3 | 4 | 5 | 6 | 7 |
| 8 | 9 | 10 | 11 | 12 | 13 | 14 |
| 15 | 16 | 17 | 18 | 19 | 20 | 21 |
| 22 | 23 | 24 | 25 | 26 | 27 | 28 |
| 29 | 30 | | | | | |

# NEW MOON

# CORN/HARVEST MOON

**30 Friday**

As you connect with new people, exciting opportunities offer growth and expand your world. Positive energy abounds as you embrace developing a vibrant social life. With a focus on building meaningful relationships, you reap the rewards of companionship and support that help you grow and flourish in your personal and professional life. This uplifting experience opens the doors to a fulfilling and joyous future.

**31 Saturday**

Newfound energy brings new opportunities for growth, creativity, and adventure. You are poised to make the most of this moment and create a life that is fulfilling and full of possibility. Your social circle expands, and new relationships are formed, providing the foundation for a bright and productive future. Embrace this time and the good luck it brings as you move towards a brighter and more exciting tomorrow.

**1 Sunday**

Uranus moving into a retrograde phase boosts idealism; it offers big sky pictures that help motivate change to improve the world around you. This planetary cycle will boost your confidence and foster leadership qualities. It deepens initiative and offers a fresh wind that spurs creativity and an uptick of potential. You amplify the potential by developing solutions that propel you towards greener pastures by using your creative side.

# SEPTEMBER

**2 Monday**

Pluto gets established in Capricorn, the cardinal earth sign. This long transit is character-building. Pluto in Capricorn encourages self-development by magnifying your power and harmonizing your dreams with practical and grounded earth energies. It also highlights the importance of hard work, structure, and organization in achieving your goals. This transit can bring significant changes and transformations, particularly in career life and social status.

**3 Tuesday**

The New Moon offers a catalyst for change in your life. Planning the path brings stepping stones that lead to a brighter future. The Mars square Neptune aspect brings gossip and scandal to your ears. You hear surprising news that feels disconcerting. Suppose something doesn't ring true to your ears. In that case, you should do your own investigating as this transit could draw misinformation leading to confusion.

**4 Wednesday**

Mars ingress Cancer allows you to diversify your interests and explore new options for your life. This transit brings emotional drive and encourages nurturing your inner self, leading to personal growth and fulfillment. It's a time to focus on home and family, bringing stability and comfort. You can successfully navigate the changes ahead by tapping into your emotions and building a solid foundation. Embrace this time as an opportunity for growth and evolution.

**5 Thursday**

The future looks bright as you take advantage of new growth and success opportunities. Your hard work and determination pay off, and you are in a positive and productive achievement cycle. With newfound stability, you can focus on further developing your skills and expanding your horizons. Embrace the journey ahead, and trust that the universe has a plan for your success. Your natural gifts and talents take center stage, bringing success and recognition to your path.

**6 Friday**

Opportunities arise that promote growth in your social life and bring a time of adventure, connection, and fun. Your positive energy attracts new friends and exciting experiences, making it an excellent period for networking and growing your circle. Your spirit of adventure and willingness to try new things leads to a journey filled with discovery, joy, and expansion. The path ahead is bright with possibilities, making it a turning point in your social life.

**7 Saturday**

Mercury and Uranus bring fresh ideas and epiphanies in one of the more positive square alignments. It brings a creative element that enables you to develop new projects and grow your abilities. It also offers social benefits that bring expansion to your circle. An experimental flavor allows you to dabble in hobbies and discover unique areas. This aspect brings an exciting energy of innovation and freedom, leading to potential growth and unexpected opportunities.

**8 Sunday**

The Sun's opposition to Saturn contributes to limiting beliefs, and this harsher transit can feel challenging. Focusing on the basics helps restore equilibrium. You lean into challenges and embrace growing your abilities. Working with your talents enables you to close the door on a difficult time, and as the chaos fades from your life, you discover a lucky aspect that draws good fortune. It offers lighter energy that anchors you to a grounded environment that promotes happiness.

**9 Monday**

Mercury slips into Virgo to raise analytical powers and provide effective solutions. Your power of intention helps plant the seeds that cultivate growth. It attracts the essence of manifestation that helps open the gateway toward growing your world. Your willingness to dabble creatively and refine your talents opens a productive chapter that brings a burst of sunshine overhead. It breaks up stagnant energy patterns and focuses on developing endeavors that advance your skills.

**10 Tuesday**

A refreshing boost of positive energy lets you pursue your dreams and work towards your goals. Personal and professional growth opportunities arise, allowing you to move forward confidently. Embrace this time and enjoy the journey as you navigate this new chapter filled with growth, abundance, and happiness. Stay open and trust the journey ahead, as it brings a rich tapestry of experiences that helps you build a vibrant and rewarding life.

**11 Wednesday**

A focus on growth brings abundance and fulfillment to your life. Your efforts pay off as you achieve recognition for your hard work and innovative thinking. It is a time of expansion and progress as you take on new challenges and opportunities to improve your life. Embracing change opens doors and helps you navigate a path of growth, allowing you to reach new heights and achieve your goals. You see a future that brims with potential and happiness.

**12 Thursday**

A sextile between Mercury and Mars sharpens cognitive abilities today. Mental clarity is on the rise, giving you valuable insight into the path ahead. Today's Sun square Jupiter aspect raises confidence and brings good fortune. With this aspect, you can focus on developing your strengths, pursuing new opportunities, and progressing toward your goals. Enthusiasm, creativity, and motivation heighten, making this an excellent time to take risks and make big decisions.

### 13 Friday

A sense of joy and excitement sets the tone for your future endeavors as you nurture a supportive network and engage in opportunities that offer growth. Your focus on personal development attracts positive outcomes that enhance your life and build a brighter future. Embrace the journey ahead and be open to new experiences and possibilities as you work towards a fulfilling life filled with abundance and happiness.

### 14 Saturday

As you focus on growing your social network, you tap into a wellspring of creative energy that fuels your life. It translates to a time of fun, excitement, and inspiration that expands your horizons. It allows you to connect with like-minded people and make new friends. Opportunities abound to enrich your life with fresh experiences, encourage growth, and promote personal fulfillment. It is a time to savor and enjoy as you head towards a more connected and enriching future.

### 15 Sunday

The Venus trine Jupiter aspect offers golden threads around your social and love life. It is one of the most anticipated transits which harmonizes interpersonal bonds and offers rising prospects of good luck in your romantic life. It is exciting to those seeking love or wanting a deeper romantic bond. The aspects of this transit are generally positive and help to create harmonious relationships and favorable conditions.

### 16 Monday

You are in a position to make significant progress, translating to a promising future as you gain traction on developing your vision. It sparks the essence of manifestation, attracting abundance and opening doors to new and exciting opportunities. Your focus and drive will help you overcome challenges and reach your goals, creating a successful outcome that reflects the hard work and dedication you've invested in achieving.

### 17 Tuesday

A new endeavor on offer brings inspiration and heightened security. Rising prospects and options bring excitement and motivation to pursue new projects. A unique opportunity provides inspiration and a sense of purpose and improves stability and security in your life. This new endeavor offers a chance to build a solid foundation and create a more fulfilling home life. Embrace this time as a chance to move forward with purpose and make positive changes.

### 18 Wednesday

The Full Moon draws a healing aspect that helps you detach and move on from outworn areas. As Mercury opposes Saturn, it brings heavy vibes into your life. Working with the energies of the Moon helps ease tension and release negativity. Personal sacrifice has been too prominent in your life. Making your goals a priority helps dissolve old wounds as you enjoy a fresh, emotional beginning that supports wellness and happiness.

### 19 Thursday

Today, the Sun trine Uranus aspect adds a dash of spontaneity and excitement to your life. It fosters new experiences and the development of innovative ideas. This transit promotes taking risks and trying new things, bringing unexpected opportunities and growth. The increased energy and drive can help you quickly overcome obstacles and achieve your goals. Relishing a new project brings research and planning; it raises the vibration around your life.

**20 Friday**

A group environment and creative opportunities offer a chance to connect with others and showcase your talents. The emergence of new possibilities in your social network may bring fresh perspectives and experiences. This positive influence can also lead to increased social activities and more vibrant social life. Embrace this time as a chance to connect with others, build new relationships, and enjoy lively discussions and entertaining moments with friends.

**21 Saturday**

Sun-opposed Neptune adds a dreamy quality to your day, having you think about prospects. Mercury Square Jupiter adds distraction which brings a lapse of concentration. You may find it challenging to follow conversations and stay on track as your mind tends to wander under this planetary aspect. It can cause difficulty following discussions and staying on track. It's best to take things slow and keep a clear mind.

**22 Sunday**

Sun trine Pluto adds fuel to the creative fire burning within as it increases your desire to gain traction on long-term goals. You enter a busy time chock-full of forward momentum as refreshing options keep life pinging on a higher vibrational level. You find the path ahead easier to navigate as new options inspire change and progression. This aspect increases power and influence and transforms areas that need it.

### 23 Monday

Your efforts lead to a successful result and open the door to new growth opportunities. Pursuing your passions and taking risks bring new experiences, perspectives, and growth. Your skills and reputation are enhanced, leading to a more fulfilling work life. Trust in yourself and stay open to the journey ahead, as it is vital to unlocking more significant potential and reaching new heights in your career.

### 24 Tuesday

Your hard work and dedication pay off as you see opportunities for growth and success in your chosen field. Your skills shine, and you feel confident as you take on new challenges and overcome obstacles. Your creativity flows, allowing you to bring new and innovative ideas to the table. Your determination and drive help you reach your goals and enjoy a sense of achievement and fulfillment. Embrace the change and continue to work towards your aspirations.

### 25 Wednesday

The Mercury and Neptune opposition helps you communicate your ideas and thoughts today. An uplifting influence have you talking about your vision for the future. A new beginning arrives, which breathes fresh air into your surroundings. It lifts the lid on happy developments, which gives you the green light to move forward toward rising prospects. Galloping horizons bring increasing motivation which inspires progress.

### 26 Thursday

Mercury trine Pluto offers a spiritual quality that encourages you to head towards discovery as you dig a little deeper into a personal journey. Mercury syncs up with Libra, drawing stable foundations and grounded energy into your situation. It brings news and communication into your life, harmonizing your energy and connecting with others on a similar journey. It is the ideal time to find a new way to move forward constructively in your life.

**27 Friday**

Your social life blooms and fosters growth, connection, and inspiration. This newfound energy brings new and exciting opportunities for growth and expansion, opening up new avenues for self-discovery and fulfillment. As you delve deeper into building meaningful relationships, you create a supportive network of friends who share your passions and ideals. The journey ahead fills with joy, growth, and the opportunity to build a fulfilling and happy life.

**28 Saturday**

You move into a phase of growth and opportunity, expanding your social circle and building meaningful relationships. You tap into the power of positive energy and attract positive experiences into your life. You become more confident in expressing yourself, leading to deeper connections and an increased sense of belonging. The future looks bright as you create a supportive network of friends and continue to grow in new and exciting ways.

**29 Sunday**

You focus on creating a happy home life as you develop new goals and prospects. Your drive and determination set the tone for success. Your environment becomes supportive, allowing you to expand your world and connect with loved ones in new and meaningful ways. Your creative energy takes flight, adding happiness and positivity to your life. Your steps lead you to growth, stability, and fulfillment in your home life.

# OCTOBER

| Sun | Mon | Tue | Wed | Thu | Fri | Sat |
|-----|-----|-----|-----|-----|-----|-----|
|     |     | 1   | 2   | 3   | 4   | 5   |
| 6   | 7   | 8   | 9   | 10  | 11  | 12  |
| 13  | 14  | 15  | 16  | 17  | 18  | 19  |
| 20  | 21  | 22  | 23  | 24  | 25  | 26  |
| 27  | 28  | 29  | 30  | 31  |     |     |

# New Moon

# HUNTERS MOON

**30 Monday**

Mars trying Saturn helps you persevere and develop larger goals for your life. Your hard work and perseverance have secured many positive results. Exploring new pathways transforms your life to a new level. It heightens creativity and brings opportunities to build your gifts as you advance life to greener pastures. The Sun conjunct Mercury aspect favors communication. It brings the sharing of thoughtful dialogues and entertaining discussions.

**1 Tuesday**

Curious changes bring a renewed sense of purpose, letting you focus on nurturing your relationships and building a happy home. You will have a robust support system to help you navigate through any obstacles that come your way. Your hard work and dedication toward your goals pay off, resulting in a more fulfilling life and a brighter future. Embrace the new changes and trust the journey ahead; it promises to be exciting and rewarding.

**2 Wednesday**

The New Moon brings fresh energy and a sense of wonder last. Being open to developing new ventures brings a sense of purpose and happiness to your life. This New Moon also signals a time for reflection as you consider what you want and what changes are necessary to get there. It is a powerful time to set new intentions and start fresh. With the proper focus and effort, you can tap into the universe's energy to bring your goals to fruition.

**3 Thursday**

Improvement brings a sense of security, helping you build a supportive environment at work and home. Your focus shifts towards creating a harmonious space that brings comfort and peace of mind. It allows you to invest your energy in developing your abilities and reaching new heights in your personal and professional life. As you gain traction, you enter a cycle of abundance, where new prospects and possibilities are always within reach.

**4 Friday**

Today's Venus trine Saturn transit is ideal for developing relationships. Expression and warmth flow freely under this favorable aspect. It is a time to focus on building lasting connections, whether in personal or professional relationships, as the transit strengthens bonds and fosters stability. Communication is enhanced, making it easier to express feelings and emotions and providing a supportive environment for making decisions that improve relationships.

**5 Saturday**

You embark on a journey of growth and connection as new doors open up in your social life. You soon link with individuals who share your passions and goals, and their support encourages you to pursue your dreams. Embracing change helps you build a more robust network of friends, which leads to a life filled with excitement, fulfillment, and meaningful relationships. As you move forward, your social life continues to blossom and bring joy, inspiration, and abundance into your life.

**6 Sunday**

Mercury Square Mars is a harsh alignment that can see disagreements bubble to the surface—thinking before acting can be a saving grace. "Fools dare where angels fear to tread" is an old proverb that speaks volumes about this planetary transit. Pausing to evaluate before acting or speaking on an impulse will serve you well today. Biting your tongue and saving harsh words may be the best action to prevent issues in your social bonds under this short-lived planetary aspect.

**7 Monday**

As you take a proactive approach, new paths of growth, learning, and success come into focus. Your ability to seek opportunities and grasp them generates a well-deserved recognition. You find yourself in a time that grows confidence and self-esteem as you discover your strengths and skills. A willingness to step up, explore new options, and seize the day draws a new chapter of prosperity and progress, where you advance toward your aspirations with grace and ease.

**8 Tuesday**

Venus trine Mars raises your energy and brings a boost to your life. You discover room to expand your circle of friends, bringing sweetness and companionship to light. An active chapter of socializing provides a fitting backdrop as you extend life outwardly. Sharing thoughtful discussions opens the path to rejuvenation. It brings uplifting energy and a chance to collaborate as you share thoughts and ideas with someone who lights up growth pathways in your life.

**9 Wednesday**

Jupiter turns retrograde, emphasizing spiritual growth and getting in touch with what truly moves you on a soul level. The wheels are in motion to bring new opportunities. Watch for signs as important clues arrive to promote growth in your life. Renewal is a theme that swirls around your situation, drawing rejuvenation. It opens curious possibilities and new people who expand your circle of friends. You soon find your groove in an essential chapter of expansion and opportunity.

**10 Thursday**

With this positive momentum emerging, you attract new opportunities that bring growth and prosperity. Your hard work and dedication pay off as you see tangible results. You gain confidence in your abilities and are inspired to reach higher goals. This exciting time in your life opens doors for personal and professional growth, setting the stage for a fulfilling and meaningful journey ahead. The possibilities are endless, and you are poised to make the most of them.

OCTOBER

**11 Friday**

A time of growth and expansion helps you find your true purpose and direction. Your social circle expands, and new opportunities allow you to express your talents and reach new heights. With a positive mindset, you'll find yourself in a comfortable and supportive environment that nurtures your creativity and inspires you to pursue your dreams. So, stay open-minded and embrace change, as it can bring new experiences and growth into your life.

**12 Saturday**

Pluto turns direct, bringing an appropriate time to re-evaluate your life. Pluto rules transformation and brings hidden insights to the surface of your awareness when in a moving forward phase. You are currently in a phase of transition that can feel unsettling. It opens to a landmark time of personal growth, which offers a floodlight of possibilities that sees your perspective changing and shifting. It brings many benefits, connecting you with growth, kinship, and connection.

**13 Sunday**

Today's aspect causes a challenging environment as you find your judgment or authority tested. Being challenged and tested feels uncomfortable as you think you are making the right choices and decisions for your life. The Mercury square Pluto transit also attracts interactions with other people who feed the gossip mill and cultivate drama, leading to a toxic environment. Mercury cozies up to Scorpio, bringing a probing and questioning aspect that has you wanting to reveal the truth.

**14 Monday**

The Sun forms a trine with Jupiter, which increases good luck and fortune in your life. News arrives, which gets a lovely boost as it brings a social aspect that liberates your mood in a freedom-loving atmosphere. The essence of manifestation gently weaves new options through your social life. Being proactive and open to possibilities helps you forge a winning path. Lively discussions bring insightful talks that offer support and companionship.

**15 Tuesday**

Expect intensity as the Sun square Mars alignment may leave you feeling restless. Venus opposed Uranus's alignment bringing growth to personal relationships. Increasing synergy and chemistry could spark a new romance or flirtation opportunity. You get a glimpse of an exciting journey that brings a cast of lively characters into your social life. It does bring a new friendship that promotes happiness and harmony.

**16 Wednesday**

Venus trine Neptune transit attracts creativity, well-being, and fulfillment. You build your life in a new direction, which helps awaken unique possibilities that transform life towards greener pastures. Taking an honest look at where you currently find yourself helps trigger evaluation, enabling you to make adjustments that see improvement occurring. The air of manifestation surrounds your life as new ideas are ready to bloom.

**17 Thursday**

The Full Moon helps you turn a corner as you reveal lunar healing, which empowers your life with renewal. It brings a new approach that revitalizes your spirit. Venus settles into Sagittarius, bringing an uplifting, buoyant, and optimistic influence. Happy news ahead gets a chance to grow and deepen social bonds around your life. Spending time with kindred spirits adds buoyancy and lightness as you release the heaviness and cultivate personal bonds.

## 18 Friday

Focusing on your home life creates a harmonious balance between work and personal life. Your dedication to improvement and growth translates to newfound success and happiness. Your willingness to embrace change opens a path of exciting possibilities, creating a warm and welcoming environment for you and your loved ones to thrive. The journey ahead promises to be a time of growth and fulfillment, bringing you one step closer to realizing your full potential.

## 19 Saturday

A shift in perspective propels you towards growth and new experiences. You develop a powerful connection to your personal life and see an influx of support and love. With new people entering your life, the walls of limitation crumble. You take bold steps forward, embracing new opportunities that let you flourish. It is a time for new beginnings as you tap into your inner magic to create a life filled with abundance and joy.

## 20 Sunday

A new social chapter helps you build stability and enhances your sense of fulfillment. It is a time to focus on what you love, develop your interests, and grow into a more confident and dynamic person. With a positive outlook, you attract new opportunities and open yourself to a world of possibilities and growth. You tap into your inner strength and tap into the magic of manifestation, propelling yourself toward a brighter future full of abundance, security, and happiness.

### 21 Monday

As you take steps to advance your working life, you set the stage for a bright future filled with new possibilities. You become more confident and driven, which draws attention and recognition from others. Your newfound focus on growth and development helps you create a better life for yourself and those around you. With time, your hard work and determination pay off, bringing financial stability and peace of mind.

### 22 Tuesday

Mercury trine Saturn adds endurance and gives you extra fuel in your tank to achieve heightened productivity today. The Sun square Pluto aspect draws renewal and rejuvenation. Pluto charts a course toward transformation and offers a highly creative part that lights the way forward toward improving your circumstances. The Sun contributes to golden beams that offer harmony, transcendence, and rising prospects.

### 23 Wednesday

Embrace the change and take action on the new possibility; it leads to growth and fulfillment. As you develop your abilities, you draw confidence and a sense of achievement. This boost in energy attracts more opportunities, further fueling growth and success in your life. Stay open to new ideas and be proactive in pursuing your goals; this will create a rewarding journey toward prosperity and happiness.

### 24 Thursday

A newfound opportunity brings newfound growth and success as you channel your energy and focus into reaching your goals. It opens possibilities, allowing you to harness your skills and talents to achieve impressive outcomes. With a positive outlook, you attract abundance and prosperity, solidifying your place on the path to success. So, stay focused, be open-minded, and seize this moment to create the life you desire.

**25 Friday**

Mars sextile Uranus brings unique ideas that help you think outside the box to obtain innovative solutions. Uranus places the focus on rebellion, liberation, and freedom. It adds a dash of spontaneity to your life today. A surge of new possibilities stirs up a sense of excitement. News reaches you that unlocks a gateway towards future growth. Life is active and busy, letting you initiate developing goals.

**26 Saturday**

As you embrace this new chapter, you grow in confidence and feel more empowered. You connect with a community that shares similar interests, allowing you to form meaningful relationships that uplift and support you. The future looks bright as you pursue your passions and make your dreams a reality. With determination and focus, you can expect positive changes in all areas of your life, bringing joy, abundance, and fulfillment.

**27 Sunday**

As you reach for new possibilities, you tap into a well of magic and potential that creates a social life full of excitement and inspiration. Your ability to grow and reach out to new experiences have you feeling recharged and revitalized. It's a time to express your creativity and enjoy the company of those around you. The journey fills with growth, prosperity, and new adventures, bringing a new chapter of abundance and happiness to your life.

# OCTOBER

**28 Monday**

Under the influence of a Mars and Neptune trine, creativity soars, and epiphanies and lightbulb moments are the order of the day. Exploring thoughts and ideas takes your imagination to impressive heights. It teams you up with a joint project that offers collaboration, networking, and communication. Weeding out distractions lets you focus on nurturing the potential possible. This aspect brings harmonious energy for artistic expression, inspiration, and spiritual growth.

**29 Tuesday**

Opportunities for growth and advancement are becoming more readily available, allowing you to develop your abilities further and reach new heights in your career. It's a time to trust your skills and make bold moves, taking calculated risks that lead to growth and success. By focusing on growth and development, you position yourself for success and open yourself up to the manifestation of your professional dreams.

**30 Wednesday**

The Mercury opposed Uranus' transit bringing a chaotic and hectic pace. The busier pace may leave you feeling tense, anxious, and scattered. Uranus adds a dash of the unexpected, leaving you with surprise news. This transit can bring sudden changes and disruptions to your plans and communication, but it can also get new and unexpected opportunities and insights. It's essential to remain flexible and adaptable in this time of heightened unpredictability.

**31 Thursday**

As you focus on the power of your social connections, you discover new opportunities to grow and learn. The bond you form with others supports your efforts, and you find new avenues to success. By taking risks and embracing the unknown, you open yourself up to new experiences and growth. Your optimistic outlook attracts positive energy, and you find new paths that lead to happiness and fulfillment.

# NOVEMBER

| Sun | Mon | Tue | Wed | Thu | Fri | Sat |
|-----|-----|-----|-----|-----|-----|-----|
|     |     |     |     |     | 1   | 2   |
| 3   | 4   | 5   | 6   | 7   | 8   | 9   |
| 10  | 11  | 12  | 13  | 14  | 15  | 16  |
| 17  | 18  | 19  | 20  | 21  | 22  | 23  |
| 24  | 25  | 26  | 27  | 28  | 29  | 30  |

# New Moon

# BEAVER MOON

### 1 Friday

Creativity, imagination, and innovation blaze a wildfire of inspiration as Mercury and Neptune form a trine today. Increased sensitivity to this vibrational energy attracts a boost into your world that bolsters vitality. It offers a dramatic shift that helps you quickly learn or develop a new area. Making intelligent choices leads to a breakthrough. It does encourage advancement as you head towards growth. You can harness the New Moon's energy today to start something new.

### 2 Saturday

A Mercury trine Mars aspect attracts a restless vibe. This cosmic alignment leaves you feeling spontaneous and ready for new adventures today. It links you to a path that brings gifts and luck. It captures the essence of wanderlust and offers an exciting journey forward. A creative aspect helps bring artistic expression out in the open. An expressive and trailblazing time following your heart begins a positive trend that expands your life.

### 3 Sunday

Mars opposing Pluto brings a drive to succeed and gain traction on growing your long-term goals. Venus opposes Jupiter and brings good fortune into your romantic life. This planetary alignment is favorable for finding joy and excitement in new experiences. It encourages taking chances, living life to the fullest, and indulging in your passions. It offers opportunities for growth in relationships and promotes balance in your social and romantic life.

**4 Monday**

Mars ingress Leo raises confidence and helps you go boldly into uncharted territory to achieve growth in your life. You are more willing to take risks and assert yourself, which can bring success and growth in different areas of your life. Additionally, today's Sun trine, Saturn, offers constructive dialogues and is favorable for making practical and long-lasting decisions. It also creates stability and supports your efforts in developing and achieving your goals.

**5 Tuesday**

Making progress towards your career goals brings positive results. Refining your approach and adjusting your strategy brings greater focus and helps you achieve your aspirations. You can leverage your skills and expertise to create opportunities that align with your passions and lead to success. Stay motivated, stay driven, and keep working hard towards your career aspirations; the rewards are just within reach.

**6 Wednesday**

A strategic plan opens the way to success. You focus on aligning your skills and resources to achieve your goals. Investing in your development brings many opportunities that elevate your career and open the door to a brighter future. The positive impact of your hard work and dedication is recognized and brings rewards in the form of promotions and recognition. You become a leader in your field and pave the way for a successful career.

**7 Thursday**

A shift in your social life brings excitement and growth, allowing you to expand your horizons and experience new adventures. With a supportive network of friends, you can confidently tackle new challenges and push the boundaries of what's possible. The journey ahead is full of opportunities for personal growth, creativity, and fulfillment. The winds of change are blowing your way, bringing growth, learning, and fulfillment opportunities.

**8 Friday**

You benefit from a more socially active time that balances and renews your energy. Connecting with people draws improvement and brings a happier, more expansive vibe into your life. Sharing thoughtful discussions in a supportive environment cultivates growth as it brings new ideas worth your time. Giving teamwork a try brings opportunities for collaboration as you get involved in a group landscape.

**9 Saturday**

Opportunities to connect with others and pursue new experiences lay the foundation for lasting memories and meaningful relationships. The new possibilities and good news bring positivity and energy, setting the stage for a fulfilling and enjoyable chapter ahead. The focus on social connections and networks leads to increased happiness and fulfillment. Embracing change and embracing new experiences brings growth and success.

**10 Sunday**

Excitement builds as new doors open and offers a glimpse into a brighter future. You step into a phase that emphasizes growth and progress. Networking and mingling bring new connections and opportunities. The new path ahead is full of possibility and excitement. You focus on making the most of each moment and embracing the journey ahead. This new chapter in your life brings growth, happiness, and a chance to make meaningful connections with those around you.

**11 Monday**

Venus ingress Capricorn draws grounded energy that has you feeling capable of developing stable foundations in your life. Improvement ahead cracks the code to building heightened security around your life. It brings a stabilizing influence that nurtures harmony and happiness, contributing to grounded foundations that provide a good landing. You broaden your circle of friends, which brings an engaging time of developing companionship.

**12 Tuesday**

A block may prevent you from achieving peak performance today as Mercury square Saturn creates challenges around communication and sharing free-flowing ideas. This aspect can also bring obstacles in decision-making and hinder progress in ongoing projects. It's important to remain patient and persistent in overcoming these obstacles. Focusing on the essentials and taking things step by step can help you navigate this transit easily.

**13 Wednesday**

An abundance of opportunities draws you into a new chapter that helps you find your rhythm and bring success. It fuels your passion, strengthens your resolve, and triggers progress in your world. A lively atmosphere awaits as you enjoy networking with friends and turning your dreams into reality. Get ready to experience growth and abundance as you move towards a bright and fulfilling future.

**14 Thursday**

Your creativity flourishes as you build on your ideas and draws opportunities to help you reach your goals. You get to network and connect with like-minded people who bring a new dimension to your life. You dive into an exciting and meaningful chapter that inspires growth and happiness. Your positive energy attracts others with similar interests, helping you build meaningful connections and partnerships.

**15 Friday**

Saturn turns direct, lifting the shutters on an enterprising chapter that sees forward propulsion moving you towards beneficial outcomes for your life. The Full Moon draws a therapeutic influence that reboots your energy and wipes sensitive areas from your spirit. Scheduling outworn areas for deletion brings a focus on improving circumstances that boost your spiritual, mental, and psychological well-being.

**16 Saturday**

The changes ahead indicate a positive shift in your social life. You focus on self-care and wellness, bringing balance and rejuvenation to your surroundings. Engaging in thoughtful discussions and sharing ideas with others attracts abundance and propels your life forward in a unique direction. Good news arrives, providing guidance and illuminating the path ahead. Investing in your talents and abilities leads to a satisfying and pleasing outcome.

**17 Sunday**

The Sun-opposed Uranus transit attracts a restless vibe that gives you the green light to try something new and different. It drives a liberating chapter that offers spontaneity as you get busy expressing your unique melody and personality. This transit encourages you to break out of your comfort zone and take risks in pursuit of personal growth and fulfillment. It provides opportunities for self-discovery and enables you to embrace change and be open to new experiences.

**18 Monday**

Today, Mercury opposed Jupiter draws a favorable aspect that nurtures good fortune in your social life. Focusing on recalibrating and building stable foundations around your life draws clearer skies overhead. It brings opportunities to circulate with your circle, and connecting with friends draws a new level of happiness. Exchanging thoughts with your cohorts nurtures your social life and brings fresh inspiration.

**19 Tuesday**

You open new pathways of prosperity, leading to a time of expanding opportunities and positive outcomes. Your skills and expertise bring recognition, leading to a productive and fulfilling journey that provides you with the necessary resources to succeed. Hard work and determination pay off as your confidence grows and you create the life you desire. It marks a significant chapter in your working life as you continue to grow and succeed with each new challenge.

**20 Wednesday**

You take your skills to new heights and push forward firmly. It opens the door to new opportunities, expanding your possibilities and enhancing productivity. You create a better bottom line and get ahead in your career. It sets a positive tone for a purposeful journey that marks a new chapter in your life. Embracing the changes ahead fosters a productive, growth-oriented environment that provides the foundation to reach your dreams and succeed in your work.

**21 Thursday**

Today's Sun sextile Pluto transit drives ambitions and sees you with an increased drive to succeed and conquer your goals. Stepping out on a lighter path, a shift in perspective offers a unique approach that draws dividends. It places you in alignment to achieve professional advancement, and this boosts morale as it gives you motivation and inspiration to grow your working life. A new project in the pipeline makes a grand entrance with a splash of color you can celebrate.

## 22 Friday

Today, Venus sextile Saturn promotes cooperation and offers the chance to join a joint project. It is a favorable aspect for building personal and professional relationships, as it creates an environment of mutual respect and understanding. This transit encourages stability and commitment, making it a great time to solidify existing partnerships or form new ones. It promotes a harmonious and productive atmosphere, enabling you to achieve your goals quickly and gracefully.

## 23 Saturday

New horizons open as you embark on a journey filled with inspiration, excitement, and growth. Your social circle is expanding, and you connect with like-minded individuals who bring fresh perspectives, ideas, and energy into your life. Embracing new opportunities helps you reach new levels of success and fulfillment. With newfound connections and support, you explore new territories and reach new heights in your personal and professional life.

## 24 Sunday

The journey ahead brings a time of growth and stability to your home life. Focus on nurturing your surroundings; you'll see that changes get positive results. Your efforts to create a harmonious environment pay off as you enjoy comfort and contentment. Your investments in personal development bring greater peace of mind, and your life begins to take shape. This new chapter helps you balance work and home and reap the benefits of a happy, productive life.

### 25 Monday

With a clearer mind and open heart, you connect with friends and loved ones to create memorable moments. This week is a time of growth where you can positively develop your skills and relationships. Embracing change leads to increased happiness and fulfillment, allowing you to fulfill your dreams and bring joy to those around you. A harmonious energy flows through your life, guiding you toward success and abundance.

### 26 Tuesday

Mercury turns retrograde, which creates a challenging environment. Miscommunication is more prevalent during this planetary cycle, leading to communication misunderstandings. Additionally, during this period, it is essential to be extra cautious with significant decisions and negotiations as delays and unexpected changes may arise. It is a time to revisit past experiences, review current relationships and communication styles, and reflect on personal growth.

### 27 Wednesday

Sun trine Mars raises creativity and highlights positive energy around your thought processes. It offers a prime time for designing areas that expand your knowledge base. You enter an enterprising time that promotes advancement and success. The air of manifestation weaves around your world as new ideas and inspiration bloom into an engaging path forward. You connect with a tribe of lively cohorts who offer thoughtful discussions.

### 28 Thursday

Thanksgiving is a time for meaningful connections and the development of long-lasting relationships. It brings about a shift in your life that moves you towards a brighter future filled with growth and fulfillment. Embrace the new opportunities that come your way. You broaden your social circle, leading to greater happiness and fulfillment. Your adventurous spirit and open-minded approach attract opportunities and good luck, helping you build a rich and fulfilling life.

# DECEMBER

| Sun | Mon | Tue | Wed | Thu | Fri | Sat |
|-----|-----|-----|-----|-----|-----|-----|
| 1   | 2   | 3   | 4   | 5   | 6   | 7   |
| 8   | 9   | 10  | 11  | 12  | 13  | 14  |
| 15  | 16  | 17  | 18  | 19  | 20  | 21  |
| 22  | 23  | 24  | 25  | 26  | 27  | 28  |
| 29  | 30  | 31  |     |     |     |     |

# NEW MOON

# COLD MOON

**29 Friday**

You are ready to experience new and exciting avenues of growth. This chapter emphasizes development, stability, and connection, allowing you to expand your social circle and find fulfillment in meaningful relationships. The path ahead is bright and full of personal and professional development opportunities. With a positive attitude and a willingness to explore new avenues, you are sure to reach new heights and find happiness in all aspects of your life.

**30 Saturday**

Focusing on home and family sets the foundation for a happier and more fulfilling life. It offers a time of reflection and renewal, allowing you to focus on the essential things in your life and build a stable foundation for the future. This focus on stability and growth brings positivity into your life and opens new doors to connect with like-minded individuals and form new friendships. You soon receive invitations to socialize and connect with like-minded individuals.

**1 Sunday**

The December New Moon brings an empowering aspect as new opportunities arise, boosting your support networks. Information and developments help nurture a unique perspective and outlook on life. Working in an assembled group brings harmony and happiness. It engenders positive feelings as you enjoy a more connected environment around your social life. Putting your talents center stage elevates potential and sparks increasing options that promote security.

## 2 Monday

A Venus trine Uranus aspect adds a dash of spontaneity and fun to your life. You can stake your claim on a chapter of good fortune. It brings new energy into your social life, and connecting with friends brings opportunities to catch up and enjoy a lighter side to life. It brings moments to cherish and thoughtful discussions which open the door to improving circumstances. It offers intelligent conversations that help you map ideas and design plans for future development.

## 3 Tuesday

Information arrives that spells success as it weaves magic around your circumstances. It enables you to attain more outstanding professional accolades in your career path. Your work is well received, and this sees wide-ranging benefits move into view. It culminates in a sudden opportunity that offers growth and advancement. Being flexible and adaptable helps you manage any adjustments around growing the path ahead.

## 4 Wednesday

Mercury-opposed to Jupiter brings positive communication and news. Saturn is the ruler of honoring traditions. Today's square with the Sun illuminates a happy time shared with loved ones, perfect with Saturn, who delights in celebrating established bonds. Venus sextile with Neptune sends loving beams into your home and family life, harmonizing bonds and drawing the essence of rejuvenation and renewal to your door. She builds grounded and stable energy around your life.

## 5 Thursday

Some essential changes are coming that can feel unsettling as it opens up new responsibilities. It does bring a journey that grows and expands your working life as it offers a highly productive phase. The new potential is brewing, drawing a path that deepens your knowledge and utilizes your abilities in an area that provides long-term possibilities. News arrives that brings a turning point as a new trajectory becomes possible in your career path.

**6 Friday**

Mars retrograde offers a chance to remove hidden blocks that prevent progress from occurring in your life. It is the appropriate time to confront aspects you usually repress. Now is the time to dig deep and look at any unresolved conflicts limiting your true potential. You may reevaluate your goals, reassess your motivations and desires, and reconsider the needed steps. It is a time for introspection and reflection, helping you gain a clearer perspective.

**7 Saturday**

Venus ingress Aquarius brings a desire to connect with people who resonate on your wavelength. Venus, the ruler of love, offers an abundant landscape when conjunct with Pluto. The energy of transformation surrounds your life, enabling you to advance your romantic life. Manifesting your happiness is on the agenda as you deepen your romance aspirations and grow the potential possible in your love life. You begin to see what is possible when you expand the borders of life.

**8 Sunday**

Venus opposed Mars, increasing drive, chemistry, and sexual attraction. It is a positive planetary aspect for singles looking for romance and flirting. However, this opposition can create more tension and conflict in current relationships, as well as indecision regarding matters of the heart. Communicating openly and finding a balance between your desires and those of others during this transit is essential.

**9 Monday**

You head to a promotion opportunity, which underscores a hum of new potential coming into your career path. Information swiftly arrives to help you chart a course toward advancement. Swift communication arrives to help you chart a course toward career betterment. Additionally, evaluating and streamlining your workload will be beneficial in removing outdated areas and keeping your work relevant and productive.

**10 Tuesday**

You can manifest your desires as you tap into the essence of growth and abundance. You attract a harmonious flow of events that bring stability, security, and success. Life becomes a positive cycle where your positive energy attracts more positive experiences, leading you toward greater happiness and abundance. The emphasis is on building solid foundations that support your goals and dreams, resulting in a harmonious balance between work and play.

**11 Wednesday**

Opportunities for growth and development arise in your personal and professional life. Embracing change brings new perspectives and helps you cultivate a more harmonious existence. Your social circle expands, bringing new relationships and experiences into your life. Taking the initiative to pursue your passions and interests leads to increased happiness and fulfillment. The road ahead holds promise, and a bright future awaits.

**12 Thursday**

You connect with like-minded individuals and foster meaningful relationships that bring growth and happiness. This new chapter marks a time of positivity, creativity, and fulfillment as you head toward a brighter future. The arrival of good news shines a light on a path forward, encouraging investment in your talents and resulting in a pleasing outcome. Nurturing well-being is also a priority, bringing rejuvenation and balance to your surroundings.

### 13 Friday

Today's Mercury sextile Venus adds a positive influence that harmonizes and nurtures well-being in your world. Less stress and more enjoyment grow solid foundations. Personal relationships benefit from open communication leading to fulfillment. Things change for the better and bring an optimistic vibe ahead. It marks the beginning of an inspiring journey that grows your circle. You land in an encouraging environment that brings lively discussions and sharing of ideas.

### 14 Saturday

You find yourself in a phase of excitement where everything you touch turns to gold. Your positivity attracts good things into your life, allowing you to live life to the fullest. It is a time to take a leap of faith, embrace new experiences, and build meaningful relationships. Your social life flourishes as you step out of your comfort zone and connect with like-minded individuals. This phase of growth and adventure sets the foundation for a happier and more fulfilling future.

### 15 Sunday

A glorious Full Moon helps you turn a corner. It signals a chance to heal the past and go beyond what you thought was possible. It can bring out strong emotions, and finding therapeutic ways to channel these sensitive feelings positively draws healing. Mercury turns direct, which releases negativity around personal and social bonds. Any crosswires during the retrograde phase will soon lift as lighter energy attracts a positive influence in your life.

**16 Monday**

A shift in your focus brings new opportunities and growth, helping you move towards a brighter future with purpose and positivity. As you connect with like-minded individuals and engage in meaningful conversations, your world expands, and you experience abundance and joy. Your talents and creativity lead to personal and professional advancement in your life. A supportive environment promotes growth and creativity, helping you flourish and reach your goals.

**17 Tuesday**

An emphasis on growth brings a new chapter that sees you expand your life into a bright horizon. Your positive energy attracts opportunities to connect with like-minded individuals who share your passion and drive. The door opens to exciting possibilities that bring balance, happiness, and abundance. A time of adventure awaits, leading you on a journey of self-discovery and fulfillment. Your future looks bright as you pave a path toward happiness and prosperity.

**18 Wednesday**

An emphasis on self-discovery and growth sparks a journey that broadens your horizons. The manifestation of your goals draws inspiration and progress into your life. This expansion creates a ripple effect that opens doors to new opportunities, bringing success and happiness into your world. Your talent and passion are nurtured, helping you find a fulfilling path that aligns with your purpose. Embracing change brings new horizons and a brighter future ahead.

**19 Thursday**

It's a time of growth and positive change, where you can connect with others, build meaningful relationships and open up new opportunities for yourself. Your social life flourishes, and you are filled with joy and happiness as you navigate this exciting chapter. By being open and proactive, you set yourself up for success and growth, both personally and professionally. Embrace the opportunities and be open to the changes that come your way, as they may lead to even greater success.

**20 Friday**

A constructive focus nurtures success and lays the foundation for a bright future. It brings harmony into your life and supports new growth in areas that matter most to you. A positive mindset fuels your drive and helps you identify and grasp opportunities as they come your way. It brings a time of growth, expansion, and personal success as you invest in yourself and turns your aspirations into reality. You prepare for a journey of development, abundance, and happiness.

**21 Saturday**

With your power of intention, you attract the right people and situations into your life, which helps you grow and flourish in new and exciting ways. Positive energy abounds, and good news lets you see your progress and how far you have come. Your focus on the future brightens your outlook and brings a sense of fulfillment. An insightful approach to life attracts new beginnings and opens the door to a prosperous phase.

**22 Sunday**

This time brings new opportunities and growth as you focus on realizing your dreams and living a fulfilling life. Your positive energy and intentional actions attract positive experiences and relationships, leading to a more abundant and enriching future. You cultivate opportunities that deepen your life's meaningful connections, bringing great joy and happiness. The journey ahead offers new and exciting experiences that expand your life's purpose.

### 23 Monday

Your positive mindset and focus on personal development bring new experiences and relationships into your life. Your creativity and willingness to take chances help you achieve your goals and create a fulfilling life full of joy and purpose. It sets the stage for a busy time filled with personal and professional growth opportunities. The road ahead is bright and full of possibilities as you continue manifesting your desires and bringing your dreams to life.

### 24 Tuesday

The Jupiter square Saturn aspect signifies overspending could bring a crimp to your finances. If you feel a bit blue about financial prospects, creating a budget and planning to repay the credit cards in time will help you balance your money woes. Indeed, choices and decisions trigger a journey of more excellent stability. Seeds planted ripen and blossom into a path forward. You soon discover the correct options, which open the gate to increasing security in your life.

### 25 Wednesday

Christmas Day highlights the importance of positive relationships and helps you grow your network of friends and connections. It leads to new opportunities and experiences that bring joy, happiness, and abundance into your life. Embrace this time of growth and let yourself be open to new adventures. Your positive outlook and energy attract like-minded individuals with similar interests and goals, bringing joy and fulfillment to your life.

### 26 Thursday

Today, Mercury is the show's star and draws a favorable aspect that nurtures good fortune in your social life. It brings a chance to share with friends and loved ones. Relaxing and unwinding enable you to restore frazzled nerves and build robust foundations. You enter a time of inspiration, manifestation, and engagement with friends. A more social aspect brings a breath of fresh air into your surroundings. Embrace this time, take risks, and make memories that will last a lifetime.

**27 Friday**

Mercury square Saturn challenges social talks. Tensions could flare up and lead to disruptions. Miscommunication is more likely when you are not on the same page as the person you are talking to about your ideas. Focusing on open and transparent communication can help you be on the same wavelength during this challenging aspect. It's important to avoid jumping to conclusions or making hasty decisions, as misunderstandings can quickly occur during this transit.

**28 Saturday**

You open a world of socializing and bonding, creating a happier and more fulfilled life. Your journey ahead is full of opportunities for growth and adventure, making the most of your social connections and experiences. It sets the stage for meaningful encounters and creates the potential for new friendships to form. You are open to exploring new possibilities and taking a journey of self-discovery. This period encourages growth, change, and positivity in your personal and social life.

**29 Sunday**

As you take steps towards growth and progress, a supportive environment emerges that nurtures and helps to manifest your goals. You tap into a positive energy flow that attracts new opportunities and growth. Your talents and passions come to the forefront, leading to a brighter future and happiness. Embracing change and being open to new experiences will bring positive results and fulfillment in your social life.

**30 Monday**

You can reflect on your progress and see you have achieved significant milestones. There will be much to look forward to over the coming months as new possibilities light an optimistic path ahead. An emphasis on developing security launches an enterprising time that brings refinement to your talents. Your innovative ideas and unique perspectives are well received, allowing you to progress and succeed in your endeavors.

**31 Tuesday**

You create growth opportunities, build meaningful relationships, and experience a sense of community. This new chapter brings opportunities for self-discovery, creativity, and joy, allowing you to live life to the fullest. Focus on personal growth draws positive change, and a new path becomes more evident. Surrounding yourself with like-minded individuals opens the door to new possibilities. It helps you build meaningful relationships and create a supportive environment.

**1 Wednesday**

As you pursue opportunities that expand your social life, new connections and ideas offer a wave of inspiration. You find progress and succeed in areas that align with your goals and aspirations. It brings a time of growth and expansion that elevates your life, supports your well-being, and deepens relationships with those who matter to you. It helps you create a foundation that supports and nurtures your life, leading to a brighter and more fulfilling future.

**2 Thursday**

You enter a positive and productive phase that helps you reach new heights in your social and personal life. You align with your goals and invest in your passions; you cultivate a life filled with joy, abundance, and fulfillment. It opens the door to exciting opportunities and new adventures, helping you explore and grow as you connect with others who share your passions and interests. It is a time to embrace change, embrace new experiences, and pursue your dreams.

# Astrology, Tarot & Horoscope Books.

Mystic Cat

Printed in Great Britain
by Amazon

35206350R00097